Video Study Groups
for Education, Professional
Development, and Change

by François Victor Tochon

Video Study Groups for Education, Professional Development, and Change

by François Victor Tochon

Atwood Publishing
Madison, Wisconsin

Video Study Groups
for Education, Professional Development, and Change
by François Victor Tochon

© 1999
Atwood Publishing
2710 Atwood Ave.
Madison, WI 53704

Printed in the United States of America.

02 01 00 99 9 8 7 6 5 4 3 2 1

Cover art by Gina Bertolini.

Cover design © 1999
by Tamara L. Dever, TLC Graphics.

Some of the experiences reported on in the present book occurred within projects funded by the Social Sciences and Humanities Research Council of Canada (SSHRCC), by the Conseil québécois de la recherche sociale (CQRS), and by l'Action concertée sur les nouvelle technologies d'information et de communication en éducation (NTIC) of the Fonds pour la formation des chercheurs et l'aide à la recherche (FCAR) and the Quebec Department of Education.

Library of Congress Cataloging-in-Publication Data

Tochon, François Victor, 1954-

Video study groups for education, professional development, and change / by François Victor Tochon
      p. cm.
  Includes bibliographical references (p.).
  ISBN 1-891859-28-5
  1. Teachers — In-service training — Audio-visual aids. 2. Teachers-Training of — Audio-visual aids. 3. Teacher work groups.
I. Title.
LB1731.T593   1999
370'.71'5—dc21   99-21016
                                   CIP

Dedication

This book is dedicated to Isabelle

I wish to thank the student teachers who permitted me to analyze, think through, and quote their reflections. Without them it would not have been possible to do this work. Thanks also to Jeremy Roschelle (University of California at Berkeley), to Gary Fenstermacher and Virginia Richardson (University of Michigan) and Paul Heckman (University of Arizona) for having shared their experiences with me. Thanks, too, to Rina Kampeas, for the work of preparing the English-language text of this book. I would like to express my hope that those of my students who have tried out video exchanges of their own will find this synthesis of experience and research useful, and encourage them to continue exploring new directions.

F.V.T.
1999

Table Of Contents

Foreword ix

Introduction: Creating New Knowledge **15**

    When Research, Teaching, and Education Meld . . . 17

    Education and Video: The New Wave 19

    Video Study Groups Situate Reflection 21

    The Transformation of Recorded Pedagogy 23

    Practical Knowledge Is Broad,
       Flexible, and Varied 24

Chapter One: Situating Interaction **27**

    Types of Video Study Groups 28

    Video Recording and the Surrounding Environment . 39

    A Tailored Setting 45

    Tailored Teaching 54

    In Brief 59

Chapter Two: Organizing Interactions **61**

    Modulating Meetings 63

    Creating an Interactive Community 64

    In Brief 82

Chapter Three: Choosing a Frame for Discussion **85**

    The Functional Video Study Group 88

    The Strategic Video Study Group 94

    The Constuctivist Video Study Group 101

    The Sociocritical Video Study Group 106

    The Personal Video Study Group 110

    The Pragmatic Video Study Group 114

    Some Important Points 120

    In Brief 121

Chapter Four: Supporting Interaction **123**

    A Regulatory Vision of Support 123

    In Brief 144

    Conclusion 145

Glossary **147**

References **149**

Foreword

This remarkable book brings together three strands of inquiry that are not usually connected. The strands are discourse analysis, reflection on practice, and the use of videotape. Put the three together and what do you get? Video study groups.

A video study group is not your ordinary study group, however — at least not when it is developed by François Tochon. Allow us to explain.

When François Tochon began working with the concept of a video study group, he referred to the activity as a "video club." When we read the early drafts of the manuscript for this book, the notion of a video club called to mind a mail-order company selling commercial videotapes, the kind that send you a card and catalog every few weeks, then ship you the "Tape of the Month" if you don't send the card back quickly enough. Tochon's concept of a video club is a great deal different from purchasing finished tapes from a catalog. It is, instead, acquiring visual images of practice in order to study them with interested colleagues.

For this reason we suggested that he consider changing the label from *club* to *study group*. He accepted the suggestion, which gives us an entrée to describing what he is seeking to accomplish in this book.

If you have been involved in the study of education for very long, you might wonder what's new here. Students of education have been videotaping teaching practice for decades, analyzing the tapes in an effort to gain a greater understanding of practice. What's different here is that the point of taping is for those doing it to collaborate with one another in order to learn more about their own practice. A video study group is not a means for a researcher to learn more about someone else's practice, but for practitioners to learn more about their own practice. Thus, the first unusual feature of a video study group is that it is made up of people who are mutually interested and engaged in common work, and who are jointly committed to gaining a better understanding of what they are doing, then doing it better.

This feature makes it something like a book study group, where interested people get together to discuss books of interest. Indeed, that is why we suggested the change from "club" to "study group." As anyone who has participated in book study groups knows, there are some delightful advantages to talking seriously and thoughtfully with others about a book you are reading or have just finished reading. It can be insightful and humbling to hear what others found in and think about a text you have in common with them. You often "see" dimensions of meaning that were not previously apparent, and you frequently make great strides in understanding as you struggle to speak the words that best express your thoughts.

Yet the video study group is different from the typical book study group in several important ways. In a book study group, you are usually studying the work of someone who is not part of the group. In a video study group, you are studying your own work, or the work of another member of the group. That a member of the group is the "object" of inquiry calls for a level of grace and goodwill often not required in the typical book study group. It is no small challenge to speak analytically, but with empathy and gentleness, of the actions of a person you have just seen on tape and who is now sitting next to you.

Another difference is that the book group can generally be quite successful operating according to everyday conversational rules, where such things as turn taking, forgiveness of mild indiscretions, and gentle interrogatories are skills developed prior to coming together as a study group. The video study group is quite different. Its purposes are more demanding (the improvement of professional practice), and the risks to self-esteem are greater because members have made themselves the subjects of inquiry. Hence, the video study group, if it is to realize the advancement of professional practice, must involve something more than a group of interested practitioners sitting together to discuss their actions on videotape.

This "something more" is what Tochon calls *video pedagogy*. Video pedagogy is what much of this book is about, and it is what distinguishes this work from other discussions of the use of videotape in studying and improving professional practice. Video pedagogy consists of linking the very strands with which we began this foreword: discourse, reflection, and video imaging. Video pedagogy is Tochon's way of making the watching of videotape instructive and productive for all the participants in the group. It consists of a unique blending of structured conversation with powerful reflective frames.

One of the most interesting aspects of video pedagogy is Tochon's provision for alternative reflective frames. He provides explicit descriptionss of six different video study groups — *functional*, *strategic*, *constructivist*, *sociocultural*, *personal*, and *pragmatic* — thereby allowing for the use of alternative reflective frames. These alternative frames permit the analysis of practice in the broadest possible spectrum, a feature sorely lacking in many other approaches to the study of professional practice.

Video study groups offer us a new way to think about change and reform in education — a way that's different from the approaches embraced by many contemporary efforts at policy making and reform. As you know, there are many calls for reform in education by local school districts, states, provinces, national governments, and subject matter organizations. Demands for radical changes in curriculum, teaching methods, school and classroom organization, and assessment techniques are being made on a daily basis. Previous efforts at such reforms have, by and large, failed, due in large measure to a lack of understanding of and attention to the ways in which schools and teachers work. In fact, for many years, the missing ingredient in many reform movements was attention to teachers. It has finally been recognized that such reforms depend on changes in the beliefs and actions of teachers and school administrators, and on new approaches to the development of new teachers.

This book presents an approach to the development of teachers that may appear, initially, to focus on a technological "gadget," the video camera. However, the focus of this book is not on the video camera per se, but on the various uses a group of teachers may devise for the video camera in the improvement of teaching processes. Thus, the words "study group" are as vital to the proper titling of this book as the word "video." Tochon's approach to teacher change employs not only an impressive grasp of the technical and ethical details of video technology, but also a very broad and deep understanding of the current literature on teacher change and development.

For years, educational policy makers, teacher educators, and staff developers engaged in a process of changing teachers based on the transfer of knowledge and skills. An outside expert would spend a short period of time with a group of teachers telling or showing them a method or curriculum that they should use in their classrooms. This approach assumed that: 1) teachers were not doing the right thing in their classrooms, 2) what they were doing was not as good as what was being suggested, and 3) what was being suggested would work in any school and classroom context. This approach to staff development seldom succeeded, as teachers did not often pick up on the changes being proposed. And even if they did, they altered the method or curriculum beyond what the developers believed appropriate.

The concept of teacher change represented in the current research literature and in this book views teachers and other professionals as experts who are able to reflect on and assess their own and others' practices, act as critical friends to their colleagues, and make changes that lead directly to improvements in both satisfaction with one's own work and the results of this work. This approach does not violate a teacher's sense of competence and collective autonomy. It acknowledges the importance of context in all decisions made about instructional change. And it allows teachers to gain and maintain an improvement orientation that leads to continual reflection, assessment, warranted experimentation, and change.

Tochon's analysis leaves no doubt that the process of teacher development is enhanced with the use of video cameras. The video camera is used for processes of individual reflection, assessment, and change, and to spark dialogue in groups — a necessary element in current approaches to staff development. It is difficult to observe oneself teach: to keep track of the responses of each child to a particular lesson, for example, or to determine the nature of the questions being asked and the form of the responses. Videotape captures these and other naturalistic classroom events and provides data for an individual teacher, not to mention discussion points for a group of teachers. Tochon's discussions of the cognitive importance of the validity of videotapes and the technical and ethical issues related to their use are particularly important for any group intending to engage in a developmental process of the kind described here.

For its combination of sage advice on the processes of staff development and of frameworks for making and analyzing videotapes, this book is at once unique and valuable. Tochon's use of real stories of teacher involvement in video study groups makes his argument all the more appealing. We think this book will hold considerable appeal for teachers, staff developers, teacher educators, and policy makers who are interested in an approach to teacher improvement that is "bottom up" and fully connected to the realities of those who do the ground-level work. The analysis presented here honors the fine minds and ample talents of those engaged in professional practice. As such, it fulfills our ideal for what teacher change and staff development ought to be about, and what it ought to achieve.

Virginia Richardson and Gary Fenstermacher
Ann Arbor, Michigan
January 1999

INTRODUCTION

Creating New Knowledge

This morning, a friend informed me that she had to attend a professional development session. In so saying, she made a discontented face, as though to say, "It's so far from real practice. It's too highly structured, and I'm only doing it because I have to." Whether as adults or young people, we have to take courses or training sessions that are only half satisfactory, that seem to be ill-suited to our needs, and that are sometimes conducted by people who elicit very little enthusiasm. Often we feel it all consists of mere repetition. And yet, from time to time, a light comes on. On those occasions, the teaching we receive seems to suit our interests, embrace our own dispositions, and meet our needs. At such times, education is suddenly invested with reality.

There is a current quest in the educational world to build better professional knowledge for and with teachers (Darling-Hammond 1996). This book presents the *video study group*, a powerful method for injecting both initial education for a profession and professional development with practical reality. (Note: In this book, "initial education" is used to refer to postsecondary study toward a degree or diploma. This includes preparation for the practice of a profession, often called "preservice education." Initial education is thus distinguished from "professional development" or "inservice education," which occurs once one is launched in the practice of a profession.)

Participants in a video study group are peers who work together to improve their professional practice by analyzing videotapes of themselves and each other in action. While the video study group has emerged from research in education, it can be used in many interaction professions — professions involving teaching or face-to-face interaction with others. Though many of the real-life examples in this book are drawn from my own and others' work in preservice and inservice teacher education, it is my hope that readers will see clearly how the video study group can benefit many types of professionals.

Educators and mentors (a "mentor" is someone who oversees professional development in teaching), like teachers, are engaged in consultation. They create the freedom to learn. This freedom, and this consultation, can flow from conversations with coworkers as well. Education and teaching do not always come from on high. People working alongside us can be helpful, and the help can be mutual. Rigid educational structures sometimes make it seem as though everything has been intentionally planned so that the content will be insipid. And yet, very easy changes could make that content appropriate and usable.

We all have to confront new experiences, and we all have experience to share. Think flexible. Be prepared to try things. The video study group consists of a sharing of experience that comes as close as possible to each individual's interests. Motivation in a video study group is unique. Content does not take precedence over the individual. It is the human being that counts, and she or he knows it. The human being must be touched. Video allows for truth in teaching. But to be truthful, it mustn't be excessively organized. Sufficiently, but not excessively. We need time to breathe.

Narrative of experience: "They were middle school teachers. They conducted some really neat activities. Parents helped by providing a video camera. In three schools, the change was written into programming, and it became their professional development plan: video-assisted professional development. They had their sense of discovery restored to them, their sense of progress through play; and in the informal exchange of experiences, video recording took on the role of an exchange of letters. Video is a lived message, and you can watch the children evolve.

"And you know, using a camera is so simple. The whole business of buttons, framing, editing, they're all quickly taken care of. It was just a question of plunging in. After that, you start to build things. Parents were so pleased to see their kids on screen. Catherine has a colleague to whom she brings a videotape every week. He gives her impressions; he gives her feedback. Using their two VCRs, they went through a whole editing process, and they organized a study day for three schools. They're now innovating in the teaching of reading, and blending that with visual arts. It works really well on screen. Their colleagues appreciate it; it gives them ideas. It's more than a recognition of know-how — it's a means of exchange and professional development."

Perhaps you know how to use a video camera. Maybe you have one at home. You've probably experienced the surprise of seeing how much information it gives you about yourself. Maybe you've even wondered why the camera is not more extensively used for education, professional development, and professional change. The potential of video feedback seems to be little known in elementary schools, secondary schools, teachers' colleges, and institutions of higher education. Possibly the only approach you're familiar with is from teacher education, a fragmentary use of professional role playing, which consists of reviewing professional presentations given in small-group situations. You may wonder if there aren't other ways to use the video camera: couldn't it be used more often, for a wider variety of tasks, and with greater freedom?

Below are a few examples of just that.

When Research, Teaching, and Education Meld

Seven elementary schools have been working together for four years on a project for change. They work in partnership with teacher/researchers who play a consultative role (Richardson and Heckman 1996). The teachers are freed up every second Friday afternoon. In each school, they meet around a large table. At the start, every session was recorded, but eventually participants recognized that selective recording was preferable. At regular intervals, progress is reviewed and discussion summarized — and that is what's recorded. In this context, people speak more concisely and thoughtfully. This approach also makes it easier to go back over videos that address the same theme.

The themes discussed are chosen by the teachers. They have to do with day-to-day problems. At every session, participants focus on a theme that may recur at regular intervals throughout the year. Academic changes are then planned.

Professional experiences are compared; pupils' homework is discussed; new approaches are brought to the table. Participants consult each other; they try to define their practices. For instance, what is reading? how is it done? Pretty soon it becomes obvious that everyone views the activity differently.

Christian observes that over four years, the concept of reading has evolved within the team. (Note: "Christian" is a pseudonym — throughout this book, pseudonyms are used to refer to participants in real events or persons whose views are presented.)

However, one change that was planned never took place. The intention was to no longer classify pupils in the school by grade and age, but rather by center of interest. Members of the group tried to pin down the reason the change never happened. Two of the teachers suggested that the project member from the university had rushed the change: "It was his idea." They went to look up the videotape of the session in which the decision was made, three years before. On videotape, the teachers saw themselves in action. It turned out it was the teachers who suddenly proposed this change: "If we're going to make a change, while we're at it, let's do it like this." The academic from the university in fact argued for caution: "Have you thought this through?" Viewing the tape, the teachers asked themselves: "How on earth did we come to ascribe the change to him?" This led to a re-examination of the issues associated with the change.

In another setting, teachers' content knowledge in mathematics instruction was explored through video (Gamoran Sherin 1995; Frederiksen, et al. 1992; Schoenfeld et al. 1993). The Algebra 1 classes were videotaped during one instructional unit on linear functions. The teachers participated in weekly meetings where they discussed and reflected upon the videotapes of their classes; some of the clips were chosen by the advisor, and some were of critical incidents that participants chose to watch and discuss.

Decision making related to mathematical concepts was explored, as were the representations used to teach the subject matter. In the end, new instructional strategies were developed in this small community of learners.

Teachers excel if they persist in being lifelong learners.

The life lessons that video can provide are so beneficial to the educational process that some educators are working to build video libraries of professional case studies (Copeland 1993; Risko and Towell 1991; Saunders 1992).

Education and Video: The New Wave

How can we rethink professional development and change? Couldn't professionals take ownership of video as a tool for feedback without having to make use of a formal, rigid structure? How can we create reflective professional communities that are self-run?

The goal of this book is to answer these questions. It consists of a collection of ideas and resources based on many years of experience with video feedback in teacher education.

The principle of the video study group is simple: It's a tailor-made journey centered on practical experience and joint action. As such, a whole range of diverse uses are proposed here. The video camera is a mirror for the process of learning and professional development. Dialogue assisted by video allows participants to plan projects and changes.

And making video use a part of education is anything but complicated. Once integrated, this approach is fascinating and reliable, and it's a process of discovery. Participants in the video study group discover a whole new side of themselves and a whole new side of interaction. Video becomes a mirror of growth.

From this book, teachers who wish to share their experiences, mentors and educators, facilitators, social work professionals, those engaged in social action, teachers/researchers, and educational administrators will be able to derive many well structured ideas for planning a video study group that suits their specific goals. We have left behind the era of generalized microeducation in teacher education, when educators received a catalog of acts to replicate as part of a practical kit accompanied by a kind of user manual that had to be followed to the letter. In contrast, the video method offers pleasure in variation. The pleasure of the video study group comes from the joint creation of a formula that suits the particular situation. It's a matter of artfully causing experience to reverberate in reciprocal and constructive interaction.

This book presents flexible principles that can be adjusted to the needs of every teaching level. This new formula is based on research into professionalism: the approach taken is adapted to the work setting. Are you keen on developing functional pedagogy centered on success? a strategic teaching approach? a constructivist approach? Do you have a secret wish for sociocritical video pedagogy? narrative and personal? (Chapter Three describes these approaches.) All of these approaches are possible; simply make adjustments according to your own needs.

This is not to say they are all equivalent, nor that any one of them would suit all situations. On the contrary. It's necessary to choose the one that best suits the goals of the group — the goals of a reflective community whose members are networking with one another — and that embraces the personalities of those involved in the action-research project. Perhaps you have still another approach to propose? Go ahead and use it. The field is wide open.

One thing should be made clear: this book is not about *media training*. (Media training includes, among other things, an introduction to audio-visual language — that is, to media literacy; the transfer of knowledge onto film; media criticism; and aesthetic perspectives.) It is about the methods required for professional development in pedagogy, using video feedback following the recording of professional acts and experiences. The book presents the new wave of video use based on the most recent research trends in pedagogy and teacher education.

For a long time, psychological and educational research rejected the study of thinking. Of course it's true that thinking and reflection are hard to study objectively. The definition of "scientific" that prevailed in this period entailed a demonstration of objective proofs. Today it is held that when proofs exist they are subject to interpretation. From a pedagogical perspective, the nature of the interpretation is as important as the proof itself. From this concept flows the decision to pool interpretations. In effect, the reflection on the interpretation one has of a particular phenomenon is itself a formative act.

In education and teacher education, the quality of personal reflection, its rigor, and its depth take precedence over the learning of specifics. Nowadays we are more attentive to the inner workings of knowledge. There is a reason for this increased attention. Teacher education centered on behavior was flawed in several ways. It focused on tasks that did not always require truly full involvement by the individual. Since its goal was to develop work habits, it fostered an approach in which such habits were developed on the basis of typical, repetitive situations that poorly represented the reality of professional circumstances, or on the basis of learning through living. Commonly experienced professional situations were sliced up into little units, each of which was worked on in isolation. While it may be the case that this type of fragmented education is useful at the very beginning of the learning process, as soon as one is in a real teaching situation, the learning accomplished proves insufficient and must be complemented with more holistic activities that are better integrated into the context. In other words, one begins to reflect on atypical situations. Because the video study group allows participants to work on real situations of this kind in a reflective fashion, it constitutes the most fully worked out expression of a pedagogy of knowledge.

Video Study Groups Situate Reflection

The truth is, life is full of exceptions. You can't rely exclusively on a simple exercise of your profession. In the first video education programs, everything was planned in advance. The underlying assumption was that we knew how individuals learn, and that they all learn in roughly the same way. The educator — the person who taught the teachers — was the exclusive custodian of knowledge. One of the sound components of this approach was that it did recognize the importance of experience and of discussing experience.

Most work published on video education and self-viewing is technical: by mastering techniques and specifying objectives, we will all become effective! But in fact, the effectiveness that can be measured through techniques and objectives is limited. The collaborative dimension of education, the co-construction of knowledge, is not included in this model. The content of the educational process is molded and guided without offering the participant much freedom of choice.

With the objectification (see the "Glossary" and Chapter Two for a definition of "objectification") of experience, it gradually became possible to leave behind these technical assumptions. We began to adopt a more "phenomenological" view of education. Now the concern was to understand how different individuals who learn differently take hold of "phenomena" (that is, the proofs of their own experience) in order to construct their reality. From this inner reality, from this representation of experience, professional action springs.

Thus, by sharing representations of action (in other words, our interpretations, as professionals, of what we have experienced), we take powerful action in relation to action itself. The reflective approach does not lead to neglect of the learning of fundamentals. These fundamentals, rather, are speedily encompassed in a properly contextualized reflection on their impact on one's actions. When this happens, those involved work together on problems and situations they have lived through and experienced.

In preservice and initial education, professional development, and pedagogical change, the reflective approach has become a major, encompassing paradigm that brings together numerous ramifications:

> It has come to the point now where the whole range of beliefs about teaching, learning, schooling, and the social order have become incorporated into the discourse about

> reflective practice. Everyone, no matter what his or her ideological orientation, has jumped on the bandwagon at this point and has committed his or her energies to furthering some version of reflective teaching practice. (Zeichner 1994, 9-10)

Everyone got on board. Different trends in teacher education ascribed different specifics to the reflective approach: functional, strategic, constructivist, personal, sociocritical, or pragmatic specifics. We will look at each of these in this book. It will be up to each group of professionals — each intervenor, educator, mentor, — to find the mode of implementation best suited to their goals and context.

Video feedback is needed everywhere nowadays. How to go about using it forms the heart of this book.

The Transformation of Recorded Pedagogy

Recording the pedagogical act gives rise to reflection. How do we act? How do we organize ourselves? How do we go about integrating the video viewing process so that it's useful to teachers? Video feedback is enjoying increasing popularity in both industrialized and developing countries. A review of publications relating to professionalization suggests that the practice of recorded pedagogy has been transformed. Whereas in the early use of this approach, the studio recording of pedagogical interactions and role playing focused on the ability to plan professional action and manage its content, the new wave promotes reflection on the lived specifics of interaction. Video has made it possible to plug pedagogy directly into professional practice.

The theories underlying video feedback have also evolved. They have followed the trends of research on professional development and professional change. These theories once focused on effective performance. They are now focused on tested competence within a reflective perspective on pedagogical practice. The role of supervision has in turn changed in a fundamental way. It now *facilitates*, rather than *dictating*, the construction of knowledge. Supervision plays a participatory role.

Video feedback allows for a restructuring and democratization of practical education. Beyond the natural enthusiasm for a new medium, one of the appeals of video-assisted professional development is that it brings together theory and practice. The success of video-viewed practice has been proportional to the limited ability of the usual educational techniques to prepare professionals who are competent within their true work setting. This phenomenon can be witnessed in the education of teachers, but also in preparation for any profession based on social interaction and care.

Practical Knowledge Is Broad, Flexible, and Varied

The video study group constitutes a new departure in the reflective approach to education. Certain conclusions were drawn from the trial-and-error efforts made during the early use of video viewing in initial education:

- The individuals being educated hold complex mental models of the professional situation upon which they will be embarking, even before they begin their education. These models are each distinct; they cannot be considered identical. Since they emerge from experience, they are necessarily associated with values.

- Placing these models in relation to one another through conceptual networks created by exchange and reflection has lasting and instructive effects, provided that the exchange is based on shared practice.

- Mental models and individual behavior are interdependent. Thus, it is the interaction of experience and reflection that gives rise to most significant learning processes.

- Since the explanations that the individuals being educated devise to explain their action and its effects depend closely on the interpretation and assessment of practical events, collaborative interpretation and evaluation within the learning group has great influence on professional development.

We are in an era of macropedagogy: we begin with the general and work to the specific; we begin with the whole in order to study events and their dynamics. The language of interaction is rooted in lived situations.

The video study group allows people who are linked by shared interests to benefit from their colleagues' feedback in order to improve their action. Every group that engages in video feedback organizes its own context for professional development. The video study group works toward professional development and change through research on action.

This book goes over the ways this new educational context can be applied. It is my hope that its timeliness resides in its contribution to the development of practical knowledge. You will find out how to focus on the user's needs by designing tailor-made interaction models:

- Chapter One presents the setting needed for forming a video study group.

- Chapter Two shows you how to organize meetings cooperatively.

- Chapter Three presents different contexts for interaction, each of which corresponds to a particular formula for a video study group and is suited to specific educational goals.

- Chapter Four presents the principles of shared supervision.

Video feedback is becoming the most significant tool in reflective and practical learning. The video study group is the venue where we can learn about practical reality — in Technicolor.

CHAPTER ONE

Situating Interaction

In this book, we report on several experiences that unfolded in the spirit of the new professionalization of those involved in education. These examples show the viability of video study groups in various educational contexts. Since teacher education and professional development are often focused on the planning of imparting knowledge and of specific changes to professional action, few measures are taken to develop competence in interaction alongside the organization of this knowledge and these changes. Video feedback offers a means of filling the gap.

The video study group is based on a flexible educational model that is founded in reflective exchanges in response to videotapings of activities conducted by participants. The educational video study group aims to objectify and conceptualize practice, and then to integrate into action the resulting communally developed theory. *Objectification* consists of systematic questioning, with the goal of bringing tacit mental processes to consciousness; it consists of a systematic information loop that increases knowledge of and control over oneself and one's actions. Thus, the video study group provides a versatile educational model with which we can learn to learn, to develop, and to change.

In this chapter I present the settings within which it is possible to set up a video study group. Video study groups are designed to order; they are tailored to the needs of the participants. Their operation is in line with recent findings in research on communications, pedagogy, and professionalization. At the end of this chapter, you will find a report on experiences in which the organization of disciplinary knowledge was complemented with a pedagogy of interaction.

Let's begin by looking at the different types of video study groups in the sphere of education.

Types of Video Study Groups

Video study groups usually bring together people who participate as they wish, when they feel like doing something agreeable. In some contexts, educational video study groups can operate more or less this way: for instance, in occupational venues (e.g., schools, workplaces), where information is exchanged about experience and change during workshops that are recorded on video. The videotapes are all kept in one room, and anyone can consult them in order to better understand present events. In such cases, the videotapes serve as a record of the different stages of development as change is carried out. Their use derives from intrinsic motivation, as with a documentation center that lends out videotapes for their educational or professional value.

In contrast, the definition of "video study group" adopted in this book includes an added communicative and reflective dimension. The point is not just to consume the video image; rather, it must be integrated into shared practice, and that sharing becomes the site of exchange.

One mundane view of the educational video study group often treats it as a training session; or else it may be designed to parallel a practicum. Those taking the training session or doing the practicum are people taking part in reflection and professional development of a practical nature. They may be students in preservice education or teachers in inservice education, adults in training, novices, or professional workers. Since, in most educational programs, these training sessions are credited and lead to an recognition of competency, the motivation cannot be called exclusively intrinsic.

In contrast to the ordinary, garden-variety video study group, the educational video study group may comprise pedagogical support, in order to ensure that participants derive as much information as possible from what is recorded on video. This pedagogical support necessitates, at the very least, a minimal structure for intervention. Nevertheless, those running the study group bear in mind that over-organizing the knowledge of others is demotivating.

Different structures exist for interaction based on video feedback. Four such structures are presented here. Only educational video study groups focusing on professionalization are discussed (in initial education, professional development, or as part of academic or professional changes). A distinction is made among four uses that depend on varying settings: the *studio education-research study group*, the *individualized study group*, the *other-viewing study group*, and the *integrated study group*. (Note: "Education-research" is a reflective activity through which the learner engages in cooperative ("working together") research into the components of her or his own professional action, while developing new personal knowledge [see Heron 1996].)

The studio video study group

Those who love their profession or the profession they are being trained for wish to professionalize themselves. The notion of "professionalism" as used here refers to the aspiration to master one's profession; to fully grasp its nuances and all the issues it entails; to develop one's competence to the point where it yields a degree of satisfaction. Feeling at ease in one's profession requires time, energy, and research. Through trial and error, little by little, we learn what professional attitudes suit us and what modes of action and principles bring us satisfaction.

The studio education-research type of video study group is specifically intended to facilitate this process by enabling participants to benefit from the advice of their peers. This video study group unites those approaches in which recording is done in settings of reduced complexity, using simulated or real presentations (with real interactors — that is, end learners — or with participants playing the role of interactors). It's necessary to set up realistic situations in the studio in order to better understand one's actions and reactions in those situations and respond more appropriately. For instance, a teacher receiving training presents part of a lesson to his peers and then feedback is given on the recorded sequence. Or, a third-year law student presents a case before some first-year students, helps them identify the important points of law when the video is screened, and, in return, receives comments and practical criticism of her mode of action so that she can improve it. A daycare worker spends half an hour interacting with a group of children. Subsequently, he can go over the scene on video and benefit from his coworkers' observations in order to improve his professional performance. Being able to see his actions on video is what allows him to grow.

Reflection in the studio enables participants to objectify their practice, plan it, and conceptualize it with a mentor, a peer facilitator, and a small group of peers. It thus becomes possible to improve it, by ensuring that there is better coordination between theoretical conceptualization and practical experience. With studio education research, participants professionalize in stages. This can occur through a sequence of tasks planned in group; a cycle, one part of which is self-managed; or stages of deepened knowledge, designed and tested in small groups as the educational experience progresses. The interactions can be guided by an organization chart of tasks to be performed, or by an interpretive model — be it aesthetic, sociocultural, or feminist (Flinders 1991). In the studio, role playing and simulations are possible. Moreover, the discussion that unfolds among participants in the studio can be recorded and can lead to joint action taken on joint action. In other words, the studio constitutes a preparatory seminar on action and on retrospection on action.

When education research is based on the study of the mental processes used in action, the goal of videotaping is to help participants recollect the thoughts they had in the course of the interactions. (Video feedback on past thoughts is called "stimulated recall.") When the aim is to analyze practice on the basis of empirical observations, in order to elicit greater awareness through a debate on the thoughts that arise during the screening (in the present), the approach is called "clinical objectification." When the aim is the exchange of experiences with a view to developing new, shared knowledge, the approach is called "shared reflection." (On video feedback as used in research and education, see Tochon and Trudel 1996.)

With this in mind, a certain university center for the education of teachers and mentors has opted for a video feedback system that allows for the co-construction of knowledge in studio. The goal of meetings is to help participants develop a professional project in order to co-construct competence in teaching/learning. Reflection is integrated into preprofessionalization modules for the teaching professions and enables students to access the complexity of the profession. The students thus develop their capacity for reflection and their methodological competence. Participants systematically explore professional knowledge, following a logic of discovery that makes it possible to individualize know-how.

To some extent, this individualization of practical knowledge counteracts the theoretical formalism, dogmatism, and conformity of evaluative approaches based on grids and diagrams. The team of workers at this center is striving to get past the stage of objectifying the memory of the video-viewed professional acts and enter the classroom with a recording plan that has been discussed with participants. Reflection takes place in two stages:

- Understanding of a specific competency within the professional act. In this instance, an effort is made to capture the image of the competency as displayed by professionals in action.

- The participant's implementation of the targeted competency.

A process of definition of competencies is undertaken with the mentors; then some quite delicate analytical tools are set up, and a process of dialectical reflection between theory and practice is launched. These analytical tools are used in two stages. The first consists of non-stimulated analysis (no screening) and immediately following this, a return to the image with the participant conducting self-analysis. In this stage, the participant may come to see that certain recollections were incorrect. She or he may, for example, have reconstructed the professional situation with the addition or omission of certain important components. The second stage takes place a week later with a new screening accompanied by a more in-depth analysis.

Action depends in large part on interpretation. Reflection on these practical instances allows the participants to do work on their representation of their professional actions, and thus engage in professional development. Reflective recall stimulates creativity and enables one to envision alternatives to the way a situation unfolded. Techniques are used to make mental processes explicit, constituting data-gathering that will serve as the basis for teacher education, professional development, and change properly so called.

The individualized video study group

Another type of video study group is based on an individualized approach to video feedback. The individualized study group relies on self-viewing — that is, observation of one's own professional action as recorded on video. Using this formula, the video study group provides specific assistance for each case. Several cases independent of each other are tied into a consultative structure worked out by members of the individualized study group.

For example, some elementary school teachers have asked a mentor to supervise them in an individualized video study group because they want to improve their question-and-answer exercises in mathematics teaching. Specifically, they would like professional development in their teaching of fractions. Every week, each one records twenty minutes of a key lesson on this subject and then asks the mentor to evaluate her or his progress. The mentor serves as the consultant and tells participants what could be improved in their approach. These teachers can consult their coworkers' videotapes for ideas as the process unfolds. Sometimes they talk to each other about it in the cafeteria or in the staff room, but their goal is fairly individual and their video study group is individualized.

This method is scaled, then, to the individual. Change concerns an individual participant. Participants take charge of their personal video recordings and screen them in private or with external support. The study group can supply materials, guidelines for group functioning, worksheets and analysis forms, and action plans. Since the *self-viewing* is conducted as the individual sees fit, the trajectory followed is often very personal, with occasional help from a mentor, a peer facilitator, or the peer group. This trajectory is founded on presentations made in a real-life setting, videotaped, and viewed at the subject's discretion.

Until recently, self-viewing was used on the whole as part of a process of professional development, whereas studio education research was used on the whole in initial education. (This is what is sometimes referred to in this book as "microeducation" — see the Glossary.) The situation is changing, however. Now we are discovering the potential for change developed in studio among professionals, and the possibilities for remotely guided self-viewing are also being explored in initial education.

An experiment in self-viewing was carried out under my supervision at the École Normale Secondaire d'Enseignement Technique de Konakry, in Guinea. The goal was to experimentally integrate practical reflection into the education of vocational teachers. This process included the videotaping of student teachers in a technical class, an individualized critical self-viewing allowing the student teacher to verbalize her or his intentions and go back over the lesson, and a fresh session in which the gains through reflection were integrated. The hypothesis the action program was based upon was that a causal relationship existed between video feedback and the improvement of pedagogical practice owing to the student teachers' process of reflection. This process of reflection was based on the student teachers' verbalizations which took place when they reviewed their videotaped lesson as well as during interviews.

Self-viewing confronts an individual with her or his self-image by means of technological mediation limited, for example, to introducing the video camera into the usual professional setting. The practice of self-viewing can be, at least in part, autonomous; but critical input remains necessary for progress to occur. This formula is sometimes used for preventive or therapeutic ends. Self-evaluation plays a major role in self-viewing, whereas in an education-research group in studio, evaluation by others (peers) plays a role equal to or greater than that of introspection and retrospection. Thus, self-viewing is defined as a process of self-evaluation and professional development centered on individual experience within the work setting.

The other-viewing video study group

The use of audiovisual media is being freed up from the recording studio, penetrating practicums and internships, building new bridges among those who supervise beginners, and promoting dialogue and institutional partnerships. Room is being made for genuine innovation. The technology in question fosters the transfer of information from the professional locus to decentralized loci of reflection. Distance education could benefit from the transmission of videotaped images.

The framework for this third way of making use of a video study group is what I shall call other-viewing. Viewing or videotaping the other in action, on the Internet for example, would fall into this category.

In the first two types of video study groups we looked at, the education related to video feedback on one's own action as a participant in the study group's activities. The third use of videotape consists of watching another person in action. To this end, for instance, an educator-researcher has assembled what amounts to a film library of movies featuring teachers. (In movies, Gary Fenstermacher has found sequences that provide good illustrations of the "executive," the "therapist," and the "liberationist" approaches to teaching [see Fenstermacher and Soltis 1992]). His goal is to facilitate pedagogical reflection in new candidates for the teaching profession, using short excerpts from famous films.

Other-viewing consists of screening another person's professional activities and using them as an illustration in the analysis of professional practice. Within this frame of reference, teacher educators and mentors seek out prerecorded materials which can be very recent.

Let's look at an example. Two researchers are trying to develop a bank of teaching situations that illustrate know-how in its daily reality (Carbonneau and Hétu 1993, 2). Since it's hard to find documents on film or videotape that reflect the complexity of professional events and enable reflection on their implications, the researchers try to incorporate a feeling for the profession into their course by means of the weekly screening, as the school year unfolds, of one teacher's lessons, commented and reflected upon. The project is called "Classroom Live," and the documentary style of videotaping calls on these future practitioners to adopt a position regarding the events they are witnessing.

For this project, an infrastructure was set up for choosing the best images with optimum sound. In this regard, the arrangement for videotaping resembles those used by researchers working in laboratories. The objectives, however, were different. The new objectives were to "read" professional situations for educational purposes:

- To identify the components of an intervention model.

- To extrude action models from practice.

- To analyze the relationships between theoretical models and the implicit models that come into play in practice.

- To identify one's own action project. (Carbonneau and Hétu 1993, 4)

Following the screenings, the teacher whose interactions had been recorded met the group of students on three occasions:

> My daily life took on a whole range of color before the camera. It was studied, taken apart, and then put back together, at the wish of people who witnessed it by means of videocassettes that robbed me of my image. This was me, but me seen from a distance. My own identity has been saved. I'm not that image ....

> A videocassette can only convey an image that others will handle according to what they perceive, according to what they are, not according to what it is. (Trudel 1995, 5)

In the course of this experience, the researchers undertook to research their own action. Their work took account of the reflection activities. They emphasized the educational impact of a realistic piece of visual material when it is associated with reasoned reflection that explicates the tacit knowledge put into effect in professional practice. Within this frame of reference, the "life narrative in education" fostered the integration of knowledge about action by the preservice learners.

The integrated video study group:
From the studio to the professional setting

Four criticisms have been leveled at those who initiated studio video education. These criticisms continue to be relevant because of the infrastructure used in reduced-complexity settings:

1. To some extent, the use of the camera alters the naturalness of the professional activity.

2. A presentation made before other student teachers, or real interactors (that is, end learners — see Glossary) who have been artificially brought together for the purpose, is of diminished value.

3. Reduction in complexity prevents full professional learning.

4. Competencies cannot be exercised in isolation from one another.

Here are the thoughts of Yves (a student teacher) on this subject:

The camera is a very intimidating tool for any beginner. Within studio video education, [the participant] tries to act not just before a camera but also before other adults. The camera and the absence of true interactors constitute an obstacle to the creation of a genuine work atmosphere. The reactions and behavior [of the participant] would be different if the clientele consisted of interactors in a non-simulated situation.

While recourse to real interactors in a professional context is not possible in a process of professionalization, nevertheless reality can be approximated. The simulated setting reassures some participants but exasperates others. To reduce the feeling of artificiality connected with role-playing situations in a simulated setting, a progressive transition toward practice can be provided by means of feedback on video recordings of real professional situations. A subtle transition is made from studio to self-viewing and then to shared reflective exchanges. Little by little, videotaped feedback is integrated into settings that entail professional activity.

And there we have the definition of an *integrated video study group*. In this context, group reflection and the sharing of experience assume greater importance. Large numbers of people can engage in the practical stages together.

Here is an example. A model of professional development has been designed to support teachers and educators. This model builds on participants' prior knowledge and beliefs. To help them to improve their professional action, the following activities are organized (Knuth and Baxendale 1995):

- Understanding and discussing the usefulness of change in order to access new methods and practices

- Learning from research to build an informative knowledge base

- Watching expert teachers and modeling appropriate actions through case analysis

- Experiencing, sharing, receiving feedback, and reflecting on action

- Evolving toward better practice through visualization (self-coaching), other-coaching, and assisted practice

- Perfecting experience and building expertise through transfer in to new situations of the same nature

The video study group can match these goals and develop professional expertise (Figure 1).

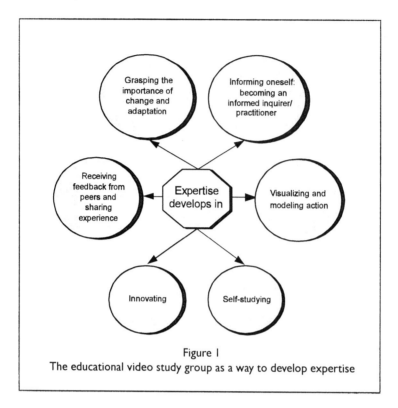

Figure I
The educational video study group as a way to develop expertise

The integrated study group adopts the best of the studio and individualized study groups. It constitutes what could be called a mixed setting for recording, sharing, and reflection. Its activities work well in an ordinary room, whether a meeting room or classroom, but presentations in studio and role playing can alternate with recordings in the work setting. The process of videotaping is integrated into work meetings and seminars to provide the opportunity to reflect on the methods of practical reflection that operate within the study group. Thus, analysis is conducted on tapings done during practicums and internships, professional practice, project experiences, and meetings of the study group. Videotaping can be individual, it can be of two people, or it can be done in small groups.

This is the most flexible formula for video study groups. The integrated video study group is economical with respect to timetabling, the number of intervenors and peer facilitators (Note: a "peer facilitator" is a participant in the video study group chosen to act as facilitator within her or his group as the group's activities unfold) involved, infrastructure, and investment in facilities. And yet this in no way reduces the quality of the feedback and of professional reflection.

In Chapter Three I will be presenting several forms of video study groups. They can be integrated directly into the educational or work setting. The video study group can be integrated into professional disciplines or the teaching of various school subjects, as well as specialized university courses within technical and professional disciplines and the social sciences and humanities. Such integration gives participants the opportunity to resolve situations, integrate theory into action, debate, and benefit from joint objectification.

In short, the video study group constitutes a new pedagogical and educational option that promotes practical reflection, whether oriented pragmatically, sociocritically, humanistically, strategically, or functionally. It is defined as a sequence of professional presentations tied to projects, the video recording of those presentations, and reflective exchanges in which these recordings are screened, with a view toward constructing practical knowledge.

Video Recording
and the Surrounding Environment

Since video recording came on the scene, video technology has made huge advances, both qualitatively, in terms of easy handling, and quantitatively, in terms of numbers of users. Today, the price of a piece of video equipment has become far more accessible; as well, the lighting problems that entailed a heavy infrastructure of projectors for the earliest video recordings have now been generally resolved, thanks to the increased sensitivity of magnetic tape and improvements made to the cameras.

When we consider the limits the first educators who worked with video cameras had to live with, we can fairly say that, technologically speaking, it is now easy to record in the work setting, and to even ask members of a video study group to tape themselves in professional contexts (in contrast to the true-to-life but nevertheless more artificial context of studio video education). Video education has thus freed itself from an exclusively laboratory-based orientation and broadened to include self-viewing and other-viewing in reflection groups on the image, for all levels of education and within various occupational sectors. This freeing up occurred in response to criticism that a sequential acquisition of limited abilities centered on performance is inadequate to develop complex competencies that cannot, in the last analysis, be dissected.

Video education was originally conducted in a simulated setting. For this reason, dedicated rooms organized to suit the purpose exist in many institutions. The most sophisticated are equipped with many microphones scattered across the ceiling and two-way mirrors for observers. (Thus, discussion groups can be organized in an adjacent room during the action, while the subsequent screening allows for a deepened exploration — with the videotaped student teacher present — of the reasons for certain decisions.) The cameras can be behind the glass or attached to the ceiling and controlled electronically with a control panel; or they can be right in the room.

 When all is said and done, however, mobile cameras on the ceiling, controlled electronically, and various technical arrangements can be important in obtaining high-fidelity recordings; but they make no contribution at all if the quality of the education is mediocre and if participants are not fully involved. Video pedagogy, though a technological phenomenon, is founded on well-balanced strategies of interaction and joint reflection that are rooted in participants' personal and social goals and in projects to which the participants are favorably disposed. The video study group relies on participants' motivation.

Lightweight equipment in a flexible setting

Video technology is light and portable. It allows for the objectification of professional behavior in the work setting as well as in the laboratory, through the faithful restoration of exchanges that have taken place. It renders possible self-observation and self-evaluation. Formerly, these were difficult to conduct and could only be performed by means of memory and the subjective impressions of outside observers. Video technology brings education and change in line with a logic of feedback and professional development suited to individual and group circumstances. It allows for the creation of communities of reflection on professional practice and can resolve the problem of the integration of academic disciplines into professional education.

The experience of recording and screening can be renewed at will, and between recording sessions it is possible to envision tailored feedback. Video pedagogy requires, however, the personal commitment of the educator or the mentor as well as an institutional commitment. In particular, the budget for total payroll must include an adequate time investment in this process. The initial costs for the organization of space, timetabling, and the hiring of mentors (based, for instance, on no more than eight participants in one group) have gradually led higher education institutions to rationalize the management of video pedagogy and integrate it, whenever possible, into the regular professional education program. With current means, it's possible to organize a video study group with forty to sixty participants taking part in two-thirds of the meetings, as their own recordings are made. The meetings can be organized by theme and the groups can adopt a shared learning approach (see Chapter Two). This format can be integrated easily and at relatively low cost into a university, a teachers' college, a school, or the work setting.

Once some thought has been given to the structural framework in which education will take place (a subject examined later on in this chapter), attention must be paid to the matter of the camera and the VCR. In general, video study groups currently favor technical equipment that is light and versatile. Excellent work can be done with a small portable camcorder. To some extent, the setting in which shooting will take place will determine the kind of use that can be made of the videotaped image. This is a matter of concrete concern. If the learners record their experiences with amateur equipment, their recordings will lose quality after two generations of prints during the process of preparing an edited synthesis. Material of this kind creates a predisposition to a type of feedback that is based on on-the-spot selection of clips from several videotapes, rather than on prior editing.

The VHS system largely prevents access to sophisticated technology because of the time the tape takes to unwind and the very poor quality of the recording. S-VHS and Hi-8mm systems represent a substantial improvement in analog recording. Digital video recording with DVD-R or a high-capacity hard disk has been designed to get around these problems, but editing and engraving require complex equipment and a multimedia informatics environment.

It is important to be aware of the choices made and their implications. It's better to ask participants to preselect short extracts from their tapes, or to make brief videos of a few significant events, than for all to attend interminable recordings whose significance escapes everyone for lack of information about their context. The presentation of video clips must be well prepared and well put across. The clips must be introduced with a commentary that explains the intent underlying the choices made.

The essential advantage of video as opposed to audio recording is that it recreates both the voice and the behavior, the physical context, the direction of the gaze. It is necessary to have the courage to shoot up close, which reduces sound distortion and background noise. Infrared microphones may be useful. Vocal expression is as important as gestures, and the reflection conducted immediately after the professional presentation is also revealing for the purposes of deepened roundtable discussion with the full group of learners.

At the end of this chapter, I present two concrete experiences. These experiences, which took place during preservice teacher education, relate to class management and supply-teaching management. The video study group allows the learner to construct her or his optimum learning space while expressing her or his main needs.

Before this venue for expression can emerge, certain prerequisites must be met. The environment must not be *prima facie* coercive or evaluative (except to the extent that dialogue is conducted about one's own mode of operation). A meeting room and certain material conditions are necessary for the work to begin. As Table 1 shows, these are the most concrete components of the interaction. In this way you determine the setting for the videotaping and the use that will be made of the tape. Who will shoot what and why? Does the project relate to professionalization as part of initial professional education, professional development, and change? What is the right time to shoot, how, with what equipment, for how long, with which group, what institutional partners, and where?

Ethical considerations

When it comes to recording, ethical considerations cannot be neglected. Whereas the recording of data on video is in general permitted in public places, written authorization is required for private or enclosed places. Informed consent must be obtained from participants and anyone who appears on the screen or from their legal

Organizing the setting	Formula
What is the institutional context?	• Preservice education • Inservice education and professional development • Innovation and change (technical, instructional, pedagogical, curricular, organizational, etc.) • Private-sector professional education • Public-sector professional education
What will the time, duration, and frequency of meetings be?	• Twice weekly; weekly; twice monthly; monthly; bimonthly; etc. • Variable frequency; as participants desire; follow-up appointment determined at the end of each meeting; etc.
What is the purpose of the video study group?	• Initial education, professional development, change? • Instructional, specific to a discipline or a profession? • Pedagogical, interdisciplinary, interactive? • Reflective, conversational, cross-disciplinary?

Organizing the setting	Formula
Who shoots?	• A technician • A colleague • The teacher • The mentor • A learner • Each learner in turn
When will shooting occur?	• During planning; during a practicum or internship; during part of a lesson or of several lessons; during the study group's meetings; during certain professional events
What is the venue for the meeting?	• A room in the educational institution; a location outside of the institution; the home of one of the participants; an outdoor retreat; an inn, hotel, or community center; etc.
Who facilitates the meetings?	• A mentor, designated or elected peer facilitators, teachers, communications specialists, learners, each person in turn, etc.
What medium will be chosen?	• Camcorder: VHS, 8 mm, S-VHS, Hi-8, digital, Betacam • VCR: VHS, 8 mm, Hi-8, S-VHS, digital DHR, DVD, DVD-R, Internet
What video materials are to be screened?	• Excerpts from master copies as chosen by the learner; edited sequences prepared by learners; edited sequences offered by the institution; clips chosen by the learner; videodisc extracts indexed by theme?

Table 1
Questions that must be asked
in designing a video study group

representatives (sample consent form on following page). This consent must specify the goals of the recording and the rights of the individual (to withdraw, to withhold personal information, or to require confidentiality).

Consent Form

Having been informed of the goals of the ... (name of institution or business) video study group, for (theme of the study group), I hereby give my consent to participate in these experiences.

I understand the usefulness of studying professional and educational interactions, and I therefore authorize/do not authorize* the analysis of my video recordings*/my narrative of experience*/my cognitive maps* for pedagogical and reflective purposes within the learning group. I understand that these texts and recordings will in no circumstances be used for the purposes of professional penalty or promotion. Their use will be restricted to the video study group in which I am participating, and the video recordings and my texts will remain my own property.

I am not charging a fee for collaborating on this project. I may withdraw my involvement at any stage of this education-research project. I will have access to all the data that concern me within this educational program, and these data will be protected by a commitment to confidentiality.

Signed on this ... at ...

*Strike out what does not apply

In this section I have highlighted the importance of using light, maneuverable, and easily transported equipment, as well as the importance of planning the components of the study group with flexibility. I would now like to discuss the principles on which a tailored educational setting should be organized.

A Tailored Setting

In this section we will examine how a video study group is distinct from earlier models of video education. The video study group alternates action and reflection within a flexible structure adapted to each group. The choices available within this structure are presented below, followed by examples of actual study groups.

The alternation of action and reflection

In a video study group, recorded action alternates with reflection. The reflection may be individual, as with a narrative of experience or a reflective interview, or it may be shared in a workshop. Usually, within a reflection workshop, several video sequences of several people are screened and discussed. Organization of these workshops must maintain a certain flexibility; in some sessions, it seems preferable to allow an hour for a "crisis" topic and view just one video sequence of a single participant, rather than showing all the tapings and allotting equal workshop time to screening and discussion.

The procedure is thus very different from those of microeducation sessions — that is, sessions designed according to the early, studio-based conception of video education. In microeducation, the screening is organized beforehand and everybody does the same thing. In this context, it's possible to bypass an event that's enormously significant within the education of one learner or to miss a discussion about an aspect of the profession that does not appear in any textbook yet suddenly leaps to the eyes of the facilitator or mentor. When a more flexible approach is adopted, integrated video pedagogy allows for the ongoing professional development of the mentor and the peer facilitators as well as the learners. It allows, further, for a progressive theorization of practice while staying close to experience. Table 2 compares certain features of integrated study groups with those of microeducation.

The differences between microeducation and the educational video study group

The opposition between microeducation and video study groups cannot be reduced to the opposition between the studio and the professional setting. It's the way action is analyzed that broadens the perspective. The argument that studio education can be reductive has merit, but it addresses only the issue of studio simulations of professional activities.

Yet, even in a simulated setting, the presentation includes complex relational factors that are worthy of consideration. Many participants are pleased to be confronted with their own image (despite an initial relative frustration) and wish to develop their appearance and their interactive ability. Does not reflection on one's own image, an implicit component of video feedback, explain one part of the success of reflective pedagogy?

Means must be used early on to organize meetings and praxis that use real interactors, even if partnerships with suitable institu-

Microeducation	Video Study Group
Theory is applied.	Practice is reflective.
The focus is on minimalist performances.	The orientation is toward global competence.
Plans are rigid and progress is linear.	There is free choice of the competency to be developed, and progress occurs in a spiral.
Performances unfold one after the other, and the whole group practices them in the same order.	The important aspects of the competency are developed in the order chosen by the learner, the participant, or the group engaged in the education-research project.
The emphasis is on individual behavior.	The emphasis is on the reflective community.
Analysis is based essentially on observation grids and closed questions; the participant has no choice but to follow the syllabus imposed.	Analysis allows for tying together the experience recorded, open questions, and reflections from the narrative of experience or peer correspondence, chosen on the basis of optional activities.
The educator, trainer, or instructor functions as a supervisor responsible for evaluation.	The mentor or educator delegates a part of her or his leadership functions and has the role of facilitating the raising of awareness.
Exercises relate to simple cases.	Experience relates to complex cases (work on major difficulties).
The planning of objectives is based on a prior formulation of these objectives in terms of the expected outputs.	Planning may be conducted by objectives, but it is based on a concept map.

Microeducation	Video Study Group
The process of education is hierarchical, and the frame of the interaction is rigidly fixed.	The process of education is heterarchic — that is, the person heading it up varies, and peer cooperation plays a significant role.
The educator, trainer, or instructor is the custodian of knowledge.	Knowledge is co-constructed by participants.
Theoretical knowledge to be acquired is predetermined and presented out of context.	Knowledge is practical; it is there to be created. Its construction suits the mental disposition and the social goals of the participants.
The transfer of theory to practice remains a central problem.	Knowledge is built on action as naturally developed; theory emerges from the process.
Microeducation is adapted to preservice education.	Video pedagogy integrates nicely into preservice and other initial education, but it takes on its full value in professional development and change. It can be integrated into elementary and secondary school classes as well as adult education, vocational education, and university teaching.

Table 2
The differences between microeducation
and the educational video study group

tions are not always easy to maintain. In general, the job of recording certain professional presentations and airing them at the meetings is assigned to one of the participants or a pair of participants. I propose to define integrated video pedagogy as the flow of interaction between studio recording and education research in the work setting. These two types of recording can alternate with and complement each other. Workshop reflection is also recorded (whether sporadically or in planned phases) to provide an opportunity for reflection on the process of education, professional development, and change that is occurring. This integration requires alternation between professional actions and reflective phases.

Clinical objectification and shared reflection in the video study group allow for the building of models of action. Learning occurs when the learner discovers her or his practical errors and corrects them by formulating fresh hypotheses with a view to future action (Argyris 1993). These hypotheses are framed by models that are constantly revised for better adjustment to the plural nature of professional situations.

Consider this observation by Ralph, a study group participant, who was reflecting on the action model proposed to him:

> The goal of these meetings is to perfect one aspect of the interaction, but when we analyze the group presentations, it's impossible to dissociate the approaches. For example, we tried to give shape to the contents by dramatizing the information. In the course of the interaction, we observed that I also based my work on biographical material and on narratives of experience. I don't think that was a disadvantage, because all interactive knowledge is useful.

The video study group: A flexible, tailored structure

To mitigate the known limits of professionalization, the video pedagogy projects I have conducted have progressed toward ever-greater flexibility, allowing participants to have a large part of the decision making.

Whereas, in early days, the video study group focused on role playing and simulations of teaching activities (in groups of eight to thirty-five, following a formula), subsequent activities were used to reflect on professional experiences. Feedback and reflection methods were adapted to individual cases:

CEDRIC: "Instead of our evaluating ourselves after each videotaping, I think that following each taping, another partner from the group should evaluate the presentation. This kind of exchange allows us to receive and accept objective criticism."

The range included in the first tailored program that was designed this way contained the following options, from which participants were permitted to choose:

A. BEFORE THE VIDEOTAPING: POSSIBLE CHOICES
Planning concerns professional activity or a project.

A1 Planning is oriented around goals with criteria for effectiveness.

A2 Planning is done for inclusive projects (of variable duration).

A3 Planning is based on concept mapping.

A4 No planning, to allow exercises in impromptu responses to special situations.

A5 Planning is done by one of methods A1 to A3, but for another participant in the video study group, in order to compare approaches to planning or to integrate interactive situations.

B. THE VIDEOTAPING: POSSIBLE CHOICES

B1 Studio videotaping of eight-minute sequences each (at the start of the first session).

B2 Studio videotaping of a twenty-minute sequence showing segments of two participants alternating presentations on the same theme, the same professional activity, or the same discipline.

B3 Studio videotaping of an hour-long sequence of four participants, shown one after the other, working on the same professional activity or in the same discipline.

B4   Freehand successive tapings in studio over the course of a half-day, working on problem solving in real cases (management of interactions, relations, supply teaching, and problem cases); when one participant has a solution to propose or a comment to make, she or he goes before the camera.

B5 Studio videotaping with interactors from partner institutions.

B6 Videotaping in the work/practicum setting (forty to eighty unscripted minutes).

B7 Scripted videotaping in the work setting, designed to integrate particular aspects of the interaction (timing adapted to the case).

B8 Selective recordings in the work/practicum setting (clips) linked to interviews with interactors.

C. FOLLOWING THE VIDEOTAPING: POSSIBLE CHOICES

C1 Screening session for one working group collectively, with examination of one aspect of the interaction.

C2 Same as C1, but with examination of several aspects of the professional interaction, the aspects being those that participants in the video study group have tried to develop as individuals.

C3 Screening session for one working group consisting of two or three participants, and peer feedback.

C4 Screening sessions for several working groups, each consisting of two or three participants, and peer feedback.

C5 An evening meeting with wine and cheese or cocktails, to screen the best videotapes.

C6 Screening using analytic grids: either individual use of the grid or group use to study one aspect of the interaction; screening using analytic software.

C7 Screening using individually chosen guidelines to respond to certain types of problems (for example, development of one aspect of the interaction).

C8 Analysis using a typology of levels of professional action and of dimensions of reflection.

C9 An interdisciplinary-group analysis of questions specific to one discipline, following extended taping of several participants (see B3 and B4).

C10 Development of practices using DIDEOR stages (see Chapter Two) or following some other model for deepening the professional act.

C11 A choice of methods for reporting on experiences, with methods varying according to the group: individual analysis; narrative of professional experience related every two weeks or at will to obtain feedback, or related at the end of the session; peer correspondence; video report; appointment with the peer facilitator; or other methods.

C12 Individual interview with the peer facilitator.

C13 The creation of edited video sequences around professional themes.

C14 Organization of a day to screen the best individual video sequences, with each person choosing her or his sequence, during
an intergroup meeting (to benefit from the experiences of the
other video study groups).

C15 Possibility for individuals to change groups or for changes to the
groups within the study group, in order to modify the dynamics
after a few weeks.

Various experiences led me to design studio and individual study
groups. Here are three:

1. For preservice education, I organized a forty-five-hour
course on the teaching of oral discourse and communication. This studio education-research project sets up
role plays based on case studies and allows students to
test material and work in cooperative — co-operative
— groups by theme. The recorded sessions are worked
up into an edited video sequence by one of the students. The screening allows for a synthesis and ap-
praisal to be made. Video feedback is also used for
group reports, which can be traded between groups.

2. For inservice education, I have designed a forty-five-
hour course on cooperative learning, offered in a decentralized format. Classroom experiences are
reported on in groups whose functions vary. First, there
is a screening, and then the group discusses the experiences. Individual experiences are re-examined by the
group using different formulas in succession. The
video study group provides a degree of flexibility and
freedom in organization that contrasts with the usual
structures; it is particularly welcome to participants
because it fosters practical reflection.

3. I organized a research-education project for daycare
teachers' professional development, in partnership
with groups of parents. By means of the video study
group, we were able to examine questions of interpersonal communications together. Meetings took place
in five daycare centers from 4:30 p.m. to 8 p.m. My

university lent each daycare center a camcorder. Turn and turn about, parents took the camera home until we had tape of each family. A meeting was held once every three weeks. Ten to fifteen parents and their children's daycare workers, who numbered three or four, attended. The videotapes would get us launched on discussions of specific themes. By coming together to take an in-depth look at educational issues, we accomplished several things at once:

- The parents were helped in solving communication and educational problems within the family.

- The daycare workers were helped in understanding each family's context, and as a result the children in their care received more fine-tuned education.

- An original action program bringing families and day-care centers closer together was created.

- The daycare workers received professional development in an area for which their preservice education had not prepared them, namely relations with parents.

All of us were thus involved in an action-research project on education and in education through research.

The terms "education-action-research" and "education-research-in-action" summarize well the operations of a video study group, whatever emphasis one may want to adopt: education, professional development, and change are subject to both research and action, and the meaning of the action is communally constructed. There is no set formula; the arrangement evolves and adjusts as experience requires. The safety net is video feedback: it elicits dialogue and serves as an evaluative tool.

It is from this perspective that the following section presents two tailored study group experiences.

Tailored Teaching

Dogmatic positions must be avoided. The integrated video study group is tailor made. It situates the professional in education research within action.

Here are two tailored experiences conducted with student teachers. The video study group component was integrated into them at the students' request.

In the first, the student teachers were provided with "weapons" with which to be successful supply teachers in classes they occasionally took. In supply situations, one is faced with the task of impromptu organization using minimal information. Often, supply teachers are confronted with unfamiliar classes and are unprepared for the situations that await them. How does one operate in such a context?

In the second experience reported on here, we worked on managing difficult classes — that is, classes with difficult students. When it comes to discipline problems and managing difficult classes in unstable situations, the video study group provides a means of increasing professional competence. Joint reflection on a problem case, taking place immediately after the experience itself, constitutes welcome support at the start of one's career.

Simulated supply teaching

The video study group in this case had a practical orientation. The aim was not to transmit recipes and techniques, but to allow for development that was either individualized or conducted in groups, as desired. This development was intended to respond to concrete professional needs.

A group of seven student teachers organized a session on supply-teaching lessons (the video sequences lasted fifteen minutes). Each participant prepared a plan for a supply teacher (or substitute teacher). Preparation was done just the way teachers generally do it when leaving a class ready for a substitute for a limited time. A few minutes before presenting a lesson, the "supply teacher" was given another participant's plan and had to conduct the class just like a real supply situation, where one receives a short plan and a little bit of material and must then plunge quickly into teaching an unknown class. The supply lesson was recorded and subjected to critique. Then the participants discussed the optimal ways of preparing for such an experience. Here are their comments:

JULIE: "The last session was very interesting. It was as real-life a situation as possible, carried to the extreme, and really practical. Practical because we often do deal with supply teaching. In my own case, the situation was close to what I experienced during my first extended practicums. I've looked back at my own video and I'm pleased to observe that I didn't seem to be rattled (although I was). We've all been through the same experience, and we can compare our ways of conducting a class. Another thing that I personally observed was the extent to which each student teacher prepared the lesson for the substitute."

JOSHUA: "I really enjoyed the session where we had to improvise a supply-teaching lesson. The practice we got from this allowed us to look more closely at aspects that are not very well explored as part of our regular courses. We discussed negotiation extensively and tested it. A supply teacher has to have more flexible expectations than a regular teacher. [He] has to anticipate holding a class other than the one that was prepared for him. The supply teacher should therefore have ten or a dozen standard lessons available to him at all times; that way, in case of a really difficult class, the lesson can be rescued using a familiar subject. A supply teacher can have an introduction or beginning to a typical lesson; it doesn't matter what subject it is, it will allow the teacher to begin the contact with the students dynamically and create a climate favorable to teaching. This approach allows the supply teacher to take note of various data (the class list, tasks, the subject, and so on). The last point is that the supply teacher must remain calm and rapidly come to terms with many factors unfamiliar to him."

SANDY: "This lesson constitutes a personal experience with twelfth-grade students. There's really no miracle or all-purpose solution to be recommended. It's up to the supply teacher to get through it and achieve good class management and get the message across. Here, the variety of opinions of the different supply teachers became a source of enrichment, allowing us to search for a strategy suited to each case."

MARY-LOU: "When you come into a classroom as a supply teacher, the teacher you're replacing often left nothing for the day: no lesson plan, no activities, no class plan. You have to present yourself right from the start and explain your disciplinary expectations for the day to the pupils. That's a very hard job. I learned lots of things. I became more aware of [the way] pupils will behave. It's quite hard to follow precisely the lesson prepared by the absent teacher. You have to adapt, according to the needs and attitudes of the pupils. Keep your own teaching style, wherever you are, every time you teach."

Managing discipline problems

Another group carried out class management exercises to resolve discipline problems. The strategy to be used was decided upon jointly by the student teachers. Before working with real classes, we decided the student teachers would gain experience through role playing, without a break in recording, for several hours in a row.

A series of cards with messages on them was prepared. At the start of each recording session (the sessions were recorded continuously, one after the other), students each received an individual message indicating what conduct to adopt: "docile but inattentive"; "lazy pupil who has forgotten supplies"; "diligent pupil who asks a lot of questions"; "hyperactive pupil who wants to go to the sink"; "passive, silent pupil"; "pupil who constantly drops her pencil"; and so on. Before the camera, the student teachers had to deal with different management situations. The problems were distributed over time, in order to avoid rendering the class completely unmanageable:

SABINE: "The session began with Tania. She tried her hardest to get the pupils to talk. She wanted to know their opinions of the new textbook. Most of the pupils weren't listening; they were talking to each other. Tania did not succeed in maintaining order. When I replaced her, I completely replaced the activity. Since the pupils weren't interested in discussion, I thought one way to maintain a bit of discipline was to have them work individually. When we came to the screening, we could see a contrast between my attitude and Tania's. I went right to the other extreme. I was hard; I talked loudly. I don't like being like that. It's hard to achieve the happy medium, maintaining control while being affectionate.

"I experienced a similar situation during my practicums. I didn't start out teaching by being as hard as that, but at a certain point, pupils' behavior changes. I don't think the reason was my behavior. The pupils were aged 12 to 14. There comes a time when they can't give any more. They're not interested in what you're trying to teach them, even if you try to motivate them by connecting with their own experience. [This class], for example, had the reputation in that school of being ... very undisciplined. The pupils didn't want to be there. They wanted to have fun. So all the theories about motivation fall apart.

"Today we tried new strategies. In this session we worked on problem solving for specific cases. When one supply teacher couldn't solve the case of a particular problem pupil, another one proposed an alternative approach and immediately put it into action, all before the camera. Everyone tried out their solution. The roundtable discussions made it possible to synthesize our experiences."

The student teachers had decided to change roles and to replace the supply teacher when they had an alternative solution to offer. They then worked out a list of rules that it was possible to follow to make the professional task easier:

GEOFFREY: "Instead of writing pages and pages about discipline, I decided to identify ten important points:

1. It's important to be very strict at the outset.

2. You have to broach the question of the rules of class operation very clearly with the pupils.

3. As well, you have to explain what the consequences of certain actions will be.

4. You have to always remain objective. Assign the same punishment for the same misbehavior.

5. Always stay calm. If the pupils see you losing your cool, they'll eat you alive!

6. Never give a pupil a second chance.

7. Identify and try to control the class leader.

8. Only punish a single pupil at a time, never the whole class. It's better to reprimand a pupil very severely in private, rather than doing it before the class.

9. Be sure to obtain the support of the principal.

10. Be very flexible!

"The tenth point is the most important, because a teacher has to be ready for anything. A teacher has to be able to make decisions very fast. There's a whole slew of competencies to learn. Every time I stand in front of a class I learn something new. These sessions help me a lot, especially the feedback sessions."

MAHALIA: "The first comment from a pupil was unforeseen, and it was an insignificant observation. I wanted to 'maximize' this comment, to put it to good use, so I turned this fairly useless comment into something positive, something useful that served the purpose of the lesson. It's a way of validating the pupil. It could be that my concern to be very clear in the things I say gets exaggerated or tiresome. I tend to repeat a formula a little too often. I want absolutely everybody to understand and grasp the principles I'm presenting. The second comment was also unforeseen. A pupil pointed out an element in the illustration that had escaped me. Once again, I had to adjust. I try not to be rattled by these surprises, but to come to terms with the situations as they arise. At the same time, I try to steer the progress of the lesson, and I'm concerned about losing the pupils' interest."

AMBROSE: "I really liked this sequence. I found it very important and very valid. But I didn't succeed at the required task. I should have been more severe. Individual bits become more important than the whole sequence, and the lesson plan loses all meaning."

The workshop that followed allowed for determining modes of operation and evaluating the impact of the subject matter taught on pupils' interest. In fact, it turned out that there were fewer disciplinary problems when the lesson was attention-getting and well prepared.

In Brief

The video study group constitutes a new approach that is less costly than studio microeducation, and it goes over better with participants. It allows people to find a place for themselves in a context of change and of respect for the individual. The integrated video study group flexibly accommodates widely varied types of use, chosen by the reflection groups as the educational process unfolds, with the goal of educating themselves, attaining professional development, and trying out a professional change. This method of exploring professionalism is new. For initial education, it probably offers the most practical approach.

Organizing a video club

Are you considering setting up an educational video study group? In this first chapter, you saw how you can organize the structure and the contents. Present your own concept by answering the questions below.

Organizing the setting	Formula
What is the institutional context of your video study group?	
What is its goal?	

Organizing the setting	Formula
How often will you meet and for how long?	
Who will shoot?	
At what key moments?	
Where will you meet?	
Who will facilitate the meetings?	
What video equipment do you expect to be able to use?	
What kind of use of the recording will this equipment provide?	

Figure 2
The educational video study group in session

CHAPTER TWO

Organizing Interactions

In Chapter One, we saw how the video study group benefits from a natural attraction. It easily elicits participants' motivation. All through this second chapter, you should bear in mind the importance of preserving this spontaneous motivation, whatever the frame adopted. Seeing oneself in action, seeing one's colleagues trying out similar experiences, achieving professional development by means of self-examination: all of these are extremely attractive. But you must take care so that the measures adopted to deepen this process of raising awareness do not harm it.

In other words, although it's good to organize interactions so that the video study group does not descend into a chaos of ideas and uncontrolled events, it is not desirable for interactions to be so highly systematized that they become sterile. The video study group arouses interest because in it, an opportunity for relaxation and authenticity is found. In this connection, the role of the study group's mentor is to support participants in their aspirations, and not merely to prevent things from going around in circles.

In this chapter, I will present several ways of organizing content and discussions within the video study group. These must be selected through a process of dialogue, and they may vary from one year to the next. Video pedagogy structures meetings so that reflection upon action is facilitated, while negotiating participants' partnership in the process of education, professional development, or change. Every meeting must be conducive to reflection on professional action. The meetings can be organized creatively. There are many ways to steer them in original directions.

Professions that educate — those in question here — are professions based in interaction. Participants, therefore, work on their intervention, and for this purpose they play the role of "intervenors" working with "interactors." Depending on the case, the interactors can be students, clients, or patients. Here are a few methods for the shared creation of a community of professional reflection. The participants will be people with a desire to act, to change, and to contribute to the improvement of their work setting. When they meet, what will they do? They have decision-making power over the modules that will be set up. How will they organize them? That is the subject of this chapter.

What follows is a summary of the salient findings from research on education for interaction. The elements presented are those that apply to video pedagogy, with one proviso: the ideas found in this chapter for organizing a video study group are intended to enable the mentor and peer facilitator to reflect on their practice. They do not constitute an "off-the-rack ensemble" that will provide a concept suited to every situation. In Chapter Three, you will find useful methods for designing meetings in relation to the development and integration of a frame for discussion. But before coming to that, I want to emphasize the pluralism and relativism of methods that can be used in the video study group.

For a long time, it was thought that what was essential in preservice teacher education was to provide a range of methods allowing the student to manage professional situations in an organized way. Order appears to be paramount in the development of knowledge. However, the benefits the learner can derive from an individual reorganization of apparently disorganized components were neglected, on the one hand; while on the other hand, the fact was neglected that whatever the organizing principle envisioned during preparation, interactions lead to modifications that can disorganize the best-prepared activity. These principles are valid no matter what field of interaction is under consideration.

Modulating Meetings

Imagine air bubbles in water rising to the surface. They head toward the air, climb, gather together and sometimes merge, and disappear once they have reached their goal. That is how I envision educational modules. They converge on the same goal, come together without producing difficulties, and have no further significance once their meaning has been grasped.

In professional education, it is important to differentiate *intentions* from *experience*. Intention concerns the virtual, the anticipation of the future. Experience concerns the enactment in real time of a distribution of what is possible. Educational modules, in the teaching of disciplinary subject matter as well as in professional education, are planned for, but they emerge only when the context allows. The modules represent possible relationships with the educational content. At the moment of actualization, they are subject to situational pressures that will determine how they will be distributed.

Let's consider the analogy of a set of colored bubbles that encounter a bottleneck. Only one bubble can go through. Until the last moment, many bubbles are candidates for actualization, but at the appropriate moment it is the environment that determines which one will emerge. If need be, several may merge.

The organization of education cannot anticipate learners' reactions or their learning needs, so educational modules are virtual. Their activation depends on appropriate circumstances. For this reason, I would suggest that video study group designers allow for a larger number of modules than what can realistically be implemented in the time allowed for meetings. The multiplicity of possibilities will allow for adjustment and for a good fit between the study group's operation and participants' requirements.

One's way of effecting education or change depends in part on her or his socioaffective relationship with the learners and their relationship among themselves, on self-control, and on openness to others. Education and change are thus both based on two opposing aspects of information processing. Intentions anticipate potential relationships with the educational content and relate to the conception of action through time. Intentions for a meeting emphasize direction, whereas the relationship among participants takes shape in the here and now and may modify the initial intentions. Thus, representation of future action does not always correspond with lived action, because experience entails a reframing of intentions.

The temporal distinction between intentions and experience is a feature, then, of the break between theory and practice, and situates the main analytical lines for recorded intervention. Modules are organized that will come into operation at a moment of "precipitation" (in the chemical sense), when the choice made among possible modules is partly dictated by context, and yet it cannot be said that it is totally unexpected.

Creating an Interactive Community

With a view to harmonizing theory and practice, meetings of a video study group take *practice* rather than *theory* as their point of departure. They then help participants model their conceptions of practical action. Participants have a contribution to make on the design of the meetings, i.e., on the choice of modules, their nature, and the way they will "precipitate" within the meetings' actuality. Some components of the design process can be assumed by participants within a jointly determined frame of reference.

Organizing meetings cooperatively

The information conveyed during the educational process can be planned according to projects, competencies, or themes. All three approaches can fit into one another. The mentor cannot design the project for education, professional development, or change in the participants' stead. Their opinion must be sought, and formative evaluations, whether formal or informal, must be planned. Since the operations foreseen are of a cooperative nature, the mentor will delegate an element of her or his role to each peer facilitator. The peer facilitator will work on certain aspects of project emergence: negotiation, consensus, and group coordination.

The mentor, the peer facilitator, and the other learners ("other" because the peer facilitator is also a learner) can choose and specify competencies using key words that define a professional field of action. The fields of competency may be written down on index cards. They then constitute methods of actualizing projects and serve as a reference for determining the evaluation criteria for successful action. That's one way of doing it. The important thing is for the group to feel that the method chosen suits the project and the participants' professional situation. It is important to maintain room for flexibility.

A whole session can unfold as the manifestation of a project for education, professional development, or change. This can be stipulated by consensus among the participants. Concession is a flexible version of the pedagogical contract and is established among participants. It's the expression of an agreement on intentions for education, professional development, or change.

The design of the video study group's program is reached in common. The intentions for which consensus exists specify criteria for the change desired. The circumstances of education are described in a general fashion, using contextualized themes, competencies, or professional projects. The themes, competencies, and projects express the intention to meet for purposes of discussion. A module is built around one or several themes, competencies, or projects. They constitute an expression of consensus.

For example, a meeting can center upon:

- A theme, such as relationships between brothers and sisters in a parent effectiveness video study group. Parents would bring videos of several key moments that their children have experienced, and the session as a whole would aim to build strategies suited to the context analyzed.

- A competency, such as "negotiating a concession while reducing the interlocutors' uncertainty." Competency in negotiating assignment of tasks in class is a delicate one for new teachers to acquire.

- A project, such as "winning the pee-wee trophy for the season" for a group of children involved in amateur hockey. The video recording of games would allow for analysis of individual and collective tactics, strengthening team feeling, and better adjusting individual strengths and weaknesses. The coach, too, would be able to include his or her strategy.

Specifying a project's themes and competencies

As the need arises, the order of themes handled can be changed and new ones can be created. In designing a meeting, it is possible to specify what competencies are expected. What does one expect will develop over the course of the meetings? With the participants, one may choose a particular aspect of the professional domain that fits the agreed-upon project. For example, the project can be conducted individually, in teams of two or three, or in a group. At the end of a thematic module (consisting of one or several meetings), "the learners will be able to organize an informative conversation by means of a question-and-answer game that will retain the interlocutors' attention and interest in line with an explicit goal." This competency could be part of a project on ecological awareness raising. Based on this, the intermediate constituents comprise necessary preliminaries. Here, for example, are the preliminaries that would constitute the competency described above:

- Start the conversation using a variety of "icebreakers."

- Structure the conversation by theme, according to an explicit intention, using appropriate questions and answers.

- Evaluate the impact and relevance of the conversation, and of the conversation of others, in line with the intended goal.

Details of the encounter must be specified. How will the groups be constituted? What is the practice time? What learning environment is planned? Management of conversations necessitates preliminaries.

Varied approaches may be tested that will allow the learners to express their competencies or different aspects of a theme without striving to put all elements that can be objectified down on paper; and in any case, are "words on paper" valid representations of action? Not before the action has been experienced and then connected to the words one uses to designate it. The effort to explicate intentions for meetings in a plan must not exceed a certain limit beyond which it is no longer profitable. Video pedagogy is a matter of tact. Reflection will be focused on one's capacity to organize with flexibility and yet maintain a consistent aim.

The video study group is articulated around themes and competencies, through projects. Each cooperatively designed module prepares the participants for a videotaped practice. The video study group is based on video feedback. The screening of the practices is the foundation of the community of professional reflection. It is possible to design a specific tool by fine-tuning it progressively. For example, the criteria for the task to be recorded would specify the learning that is to be accomplished. They can then be transferred to an evaluation card that will underpin discussion during meetings (see Table 3).

Meeting about contact	Learner	Mentor
Beginning an informative conversation:		
• The theme is clearly introduced • Attention is captured with the broaching of the topic • The information is tied together in the recaps	+ +	—

Table 3
Evaluation card

The preparation card for recorded interventions may be designed on the basis of a concept map or following a jointly determined model that can be fine-tuned as the sessions progress. It is recommended that evaluation activities be assigned to participants in the group. Learners can also use such cards for self-evaluation when they prescreen their videos.

Focusing attention on personal reflection

The video study group is "playfully educational": it is based on participants' spontaneous interest in their own experience in their professional growth. It is self-managed by peer facilitators chosen by their groups and working under the overall responsibility of a mentor. It should not be expected that a majority of participants, let alone all of them, should reach a given threshold of success in order to go on to other professional aspects or themes. Such an approach would create a predisposition to organize education or change in terms of constraints rather than personal accomplishments, and that way of thinking risks obstructing spontaneous expression, which is needed if one is to give the best of oneself in professional relationships as well as in group reflection.

Video feedback in itself constitutes an effective means of evaluation (and self-evaluation), but that is not where the emphasis lies. Certainly there is no need to add further evaluation. Work on task criteria is conducted with the goal of reflection, not attaining qualifications. (Note: If a video study group forms a part of an educational program leading to a diploma, it's better to treat it as a pass/fail course with no grades. Those who don't achieve the fundamentals of professional competency can enroll again the following year.) In the video study group, qualification is born of personal experience and shared reflection. Any evaluation conducted derives from common sense, and the emphasis is on the correct assessment of situations and the appropriateness of the chosen mode of interaction, rather than on the application of rigid, prescribed precepts.

In reflective education, the teaching content is interwoven with interactive situations. The transposition of knowledge in the professional context occurs on the basis of extensive knowledge of the field, not on the basis of simplified models of professional reality. This transposition cannot be prefabricated. Indeed, when it is prefabricated, and those being educated are told what to do in the light of mechanisms unearthed by research, the transposition of knowledge presents a dual problem. First, it is constituted through a set of decontextualized tactical bags of tricks, and second, it bases education on the inculcation of models. This hierarchical, top-down approach to education and change has proven to be partly inadequate (Fullan and Watson 1991).

In contrast, the reflective approach takes account of individuals' representations and launches a direct dialogue between educators/researchers and practitioners. This dialogue pertains to concrete cases and video clips as well as critical discussion of imaginable models. That is the approach recommended here. Thus, the information presented here is aimed to equip reflection, rather than impose a way of seeing.

DIDEOR: The stages of video pedagogy

A video study group's program brings together within modules themes, competencies, and projects that are professionally useful. Their enactment activates various discursive operations within differentiated workshops. The success of the workshops can be co-managed using work maps that specify the features and the nature of the task. This joint and multiple design process adjusts to the various events that occur during the educational process.

This structure fits into a larger whole that includes stages for deepened education. Among the various means for providing depth are the stages of *DIDEOR*: *DI*alogue, *D*emonstration, *E*xperience, *O*bjectification, and *R*einvestment. These stages can be worked on singly or in groups, at different times or consecutively.

Dialogue is intended to create consensus on the criteria for accomplishing the themes and competency development upon which the targeted professional project is based. Participants are placed in a situation; the peer facilitator presents an anecdote or example and then discusses the competency criteria that would allow for a judgment as to whether the chosen project has been accomplished. The peer facilitator then relates the new knowledge to experience the participants have already acquired.

This would typically be the case when change or a new aspect of competency in interaction is being embarked upon, whether individually or by a group. This stage of dialogue on the nature of the project, the competencies targeted, and the themes broached elicits participants' attention to the evaluative criteria. It allows them to come to an agreement on procedures to follow and to ask questions if anything is unclear. Dialogue corresponds to the "what" and the "how" of the educational process.

Next comes the *demonstration* stage. Demonstration goes beyond words and allows action to be modeled. The mentor either serves as a model or uses a video clip that demonstrates the action designated through instructions during the dialogue stage. A participant may also try incorporating the instructions in action and showing others how it's done. The demonstration stage allows for an assurance that the criteria the group has agreed upon are understood.

The participants may then go on to *experience*, whether in a group or individually. They will be testing what was planned in the educational module, using methods designed through dialogue. The video-taped experience will serve as a demonstration for other members of the group, who will each practice following the instructions that emerge from dialogue.

These three stages (dialogue, demonstration, and experience) are followed by an *objectification* stage. Objectification refers to the learner's introspective activity while observing her or his learning. Using questions, the mentor organizes a workshop based on video recordings. With the participants in their own groups, the peer facilitators choose clips of videotaped practice and initiate debate on an aspect of the theme, the targeted competency, or the project. The peer facilitators could also suggest that participants themselves choose one or two clips to suit a theme emerging from the experience.

Objectification links together knowledge and allows for the reframing of preconceptions. *Reinvestment* of knowledge in new fields then occurs quite naturally. Objectification is an essential aspect of knowledge transfer. Through successive deepening processes, it elicits reinvestment and integrates knowledge. The reinvestment stage consists of integrating the knowledge acquired into a new field or a new practice.

The stages of DIDEOR constitute a means of organizing experience and reflection within the video study group's meetings.

Making use of professional discourse types

It's possible to broach video pedagogy through discourse. Some of the video study group's meetings can be focused on professional discourse. Within each profession, various discourse types are appropriate to various interaction situations. The use of appropriate discourse can help participants fill interactional roles. Participants can try out various discourse types in quasi-professional situations or analyze their own discourse during brief interactions, and receive feedback on their presentations in view of improving them.

The peer facilitator can choose a discursive approach on which to base the design of modules for meetings. It's not necessary to go into the details of discursive typologies here; their exploration has been extensive, including an examination of their impact on education. The Jakobsonian discourse functions (centered upon the sender, the receiver, the message, the channel, and the code) fit well with situational discourse. They can be worked on in video pedagogy as methods of professional interaction.

Let's look at some examples. *Expressive* professional discourse is focused on the person who is expressing herself or himself. In this instance, professional discourse is characterized by emotion, feelings, and the expression of opinions. Learners identify their professional opinions by organizing their reasons, to clarify the feelings underlying them.*Informative* professional discourse has a referential function. It represents professional facts without taking a position. Here, learners draw attention to the neutrality and objectivity of their reports, the clear statement of the subject and its context, and the relevance of the information.

Persuasive professional discourse aims to persuade the interlocutor to act or think in a certain manner. Here, speech acts. The active dimension of discourse is put to use. Learners encourage their interlocutors to act, using arguments suited to the professional situation. In backing up the argument, learners line up credible justifications and tie examples in with their persuasive strategies.

In the practice of a profession, one may also have to employ a *ludico-poetic* discourse. In such a case, discourse is focused on stylistic play, form, and euphony. The emphasis, progression, and placement of the voice are used for stylistic effect. Language can become narrative when a professional makes use of the world of the imagination and produces fiction. In such circumstances, narrative may be integrated into professional discourse. Learners characterize individuals, set the scene for situations, work out a scenario, and develop a time scheme, all providing a frame for an anecdote.

All of these functions of professional discourse are part of the toolkit of interaction professionals. In practice, these functions are integrated with one another. During training, however, one can practice by making a particular function predominate for a specific goal, be it expressive, persuasive, or narrative. By combining the organization of meetings with the functions of discourse and the other areas of professional activity, a group can jointly design a variety of activities. During the video feedback process, the group could pay specific attention to the accomplishment of a particular discursive function. To what extent did the participant develop the potential offered by the functions of professional discourse types?

Creating interaction effects

Once the professional relationship has been mastered, a workshop can be dedicated to the content of interactions, their nuances, and their pragmatic effects. For instance, pedagogical workshops can be designed creatively, along the lines of a writing workshop. Lead off using key words such as "evaluation," "motivation," and "cooperation," and get dialogue going among the participants. It's acceptable for the dialogue to be digressive at the start and then to get progressively more focused on criteria for a successful action.

Keep it going by using professional proverbs and saws — such as, "A teacher shouldn't smile before Christmas" — to get debate going. Next comes *WOPPL* (*WO*rkshop for *P*otential *P*rofessional *L*earning). This consists of doing skits on professional situations that reflect various work atmospheres. For each skit, a specific genre would be adopted: nostalgic interaction, surrealistic interaction, playful interaction, and so on. In this way, the video study group functions as a professionalization workshop but includes humor. All of this can lead up to role playing, another form of practice. Thus, while relaxing and engaging in the skit, the learner acquires competence in impromptu interaction. Participants become actors within the situation and develop professional ease by losing themselves in the action.

The workshop can spend time working out definitions of concepts, working on snowball effects by magnifying some professional event or some planning process, and by practicing the relationship in question through onomatopoeia or gesture. Participants can also practice elocution, the presentation of knowledge, and subject-matter memory. Or, the workshop can be used to bring dialogue about this and that to life, and to then engage in critical, systematic peer analysis of it.

The pedagogical workshop can complete uncompleted narratives of experience, fill in blanks, transform a student so that a teaching event can be re-examined in a different light, work with photographs, provide exercise on problem situations, set obstacle objectives for itself, and provide practice in pedagogical association by bringing together a teaching candidate's instructional situations and determining that person's pedagogical profile. Pedagogical dialogues can be reviewed, corrected, improved, and played out by the group. Chains of pedagogical situations can be created, using a set of playing cards to offer strategic choices. These activities can take place in the studio and lead to challenges to be set for the practicum class.

The workshop allows for study of persuasive interactional effects that can be practiced before the camera. (Note: This passage is inspired by the discursive effects described by Bellenger [1981] and in Roche, Guiguet, and Volz [1989].) A professional effect must correspond to each stylistic effect. For example, in order to produce a *competence effect*, participants should support their arguments with facts, examples, and figures, and practice entrenching their credibility. Following a research stage, participants might wish to create a surprise *solution effect*, which creates an impact and wins over the audience by turning a situation upside down. They might elicit argument by using the *doubt effect*, nuancing their position, making use of contrast and opposition, being skeptical of excessively simple arguments, and presenting inverted hypotheses, so that the interlocutors can envision alternative outcomes for the problems presented and can appropriate the knowledge and their right to decision making.

Using the *complicity effect*, participants will win the attention of targeted interlocutors ("Linda will surely agree that ..."). This works more effectively than the *intimidation effect*, which renders situations more dramatic. Participants can involve the listeners in their discourse and reduce the distance between them by means of the *involvement effect*, only to demonstrate abruptly that that distance did exist. Another professional effect, the *goodwill effect*, conveys the impression that the most interesting propositions come from the interlocutor, and that the intervenor merely complies with them. This can be achieved without making abusive use of the *emotional effect*, by means of which one can rouse the interactors by striking a sensitive chord. The *insistence effect* can be effective because it triggers interlocutors' memories. The *role model effect* presents a model and conveys the sense that the way is open, and has been made easy, for others to achieve personal goals.

Finally, the *spokesperson effect* leads one to speak in the name of the group (or of certain interlocutors); the *principled effect* makes it clear that standards and constraints cannot be avoided; and the *good faith effect* calls upon the interlocutors to act as witnesses. The *evidence effect* extrapolates a law on the basis of a single case, and the *method effect* tosses out to the interlocutors a methodical recitation of hierarchically structured ideas. Properly used, these pragmatic effects are valuable in interaction and produce professional effects.

The educational video study group allows one to create harmony in professional relations by practicing crescendo and diminuendo, appoggiaturas, and chords. In reflecting upon the ways their practice can vary, participants may address a fictional letter to the interlocutors, stage a dramatic moment, share personal poetry, suggest a mythology of relationships, or verbalize their inner monologues, in order to better get dialogue going.

These professional devices may not be indispensable, but whoever masters them is assured of being at ease during interactions and of having better control over situations. It's true that every effect must be suited to the context and to the personality of the participant. Means like these can aid in achieving distance from professional conflicts. Many learners feel ill-equipped to handle the subtleties of interactions, because little has been said to them about the role played by negotiation in human relations. And when everything seems to consist of the unspoken, it is important to bring one's own presuppositions to light and make them known. Once the relationship is authentic, work will begin. That relationship, however, must constantly be rebuilt.

Differentiating the video study group's workshops

How can the workshops within a video study group be differentiated from each other? Here's one example from university teaching.

Lilian teaches young archaeologists. She has made a video of a particular excavation, beginning with the finding of the site, the choice of places for test pits, the demonstration of how to dig, the site of artifacts *in situ* (their location within the site, stratigraphic level, contextual information), and the labeling of the artifacts.

In their university course, after watching the video, the students are called upon to express their views of the choices made every time a decision is made. Lilian combines other-viewing (the viewing of the video she has made) with practical work and group feedback on the students' work. To do this, she uses a table of workshops drawn up on bristol board. After consulting the students on their difficulties, she determines the kinds of work to be dealt with and the workshops that will deal with them.

On the table, six columns correspond to six workshop themes, and one row is assigned to each student. The workshop themes are:

- Site survey
- Excavation and stratigraphy
- Three-dimensional location of material
- Preparation
- Material typology
- Identification of sex, based on bones found

Each student has six name cards, and each cell of the table has a slot into which these name cards can be slipped. All six workshops are given each week, and each week the student attends a different workshop. When a student completes a given workshop, Lilian slips the individual's card into a cell of the table, having recorded on it her observations and evaluation. In this way, at any given time, she knows what the students have accomplished, and the latter too can situate themselves.

Videotaped practice is screened for group viewing to deepen the knowledge of the practical concepts explored. Thus, a video study group can be organized in a practical, laboratory situation. Presentations are recorded and then participants get together in different theme workshops. The feedback deals with the components of each workshop.

Here's another example of how workshops can be differentiated. Paul has planned for a set of six workshops for lower-elementary-school teachers, to run concurrently. Each workshop topic is to be offered six times, with changing content. One topic is knowledge building through play, another the adjustment of social-integration difficulties, a third timetabling, a fourth managing creative activities. A discussion workshop and a workshop for creating new materials are also planned.

The workshops are color-coded: for each topic, a limited number of admission cards of a specific color have been prepared. Participants may take the workshops in any order, and they gain admission by requesting a card of the appropriate color and taking it to the workshop.

In each workshop, roles are assigned to participants. One such role is to videotape interactions at certain key moments in the work. At the end of a workshop, participants turn in their cards and take new ones of a different color. The previous card is stamped. Paul thus knows, at any given time, how many people have attended each workshop. Evaluations are recorded as the workshops unfold. Group composition changes as participants complete workshops and begin new ones. The duration of each workshop is prescribed (some last double time).

In each workshop, practical sessions alternate with screening periods, which allow for correction of inadequate practice and for reflection on optimal strategies. For the creative workshops, the screening times serve as brainstorming sessions. The participants are required to take all the long workshops and choose from the others as time allows. Each group then reviews and analyzes its own actions on video and has the opportunity to compare them with those of other groups.

Finally, here, presented in detail, is the organization of a video study group integrated into professional development for early-childhood educators (Table 4). The organization of the workshops differentiates them according to the theme, targeted competency, and project assigned to them.

Video study group for early-childhood education	+
Project	Integrating intercultural action into a daycare and service center
Targeted competencies	A. Become aware of unwitting exclusion B. Struggle against prejudice C. Help victims of racism These competencies will be developed under each theme.
Themes addressed	1. Cultural discipline and values 2. Meals 3. Toilet training 4. Attitudes toward toys and their use 5. The teachers' relationships with parents There are two meetings per theme.
Process for deepening knowledge	DIDEOR
Dialogue	The participants collaborate to plan their mode of work.
Demonstration	During the first meeting on each theme, the peer facilitator demonstrates each of the three targeted competencies in relationship to the theme of the day. During the second meeting for each theme, videotapes made by the participants serve as demonstrations.
Experience	During the first meeting on each theme, participants stage a role-playing scene that uses a situation calling upon the targeted competency. For the subsequent meeting, participants return with a video report on the theme addressed, made in their own daycare center.

Video study group for early-childhood education	+
Objectification	During the first meeting for each theme, the role playing is videotaped and the group goes over the simulated presentations. The second meeting on each theme takes the form of a debate on methods for the development of the targeted intercultural competencies in a daycare setting.
Reinvestment	Before beginning on the following theme, participants integrate their new competency into a specific action within their work setting. As well, they sensitize their coworkers to the type of situation in question. They give an account of this reinvestment in a brief report distributed to other participants. These reports will constitute a bank of new ideas.
Work on discourse	During the dialogue stage, participants are requested to recount their experiences in narrative form. During the objectification stage, they try to clarify their perceptions by going from the expressive discourse associated with emotions to the informative discourse that is based on facts.
Interaction effects	As they carry out their work in daycare, in order to sensitize the children to the intercultural dimension of their situation, the participants deploy the emotional effect and the solution effect, using concrete cases. Thus, they make themselves more easily understood.
Shared organization	The participants divide responsibility for the five themes, assigning each to a pair of participants. So for each theme, two participants are considered experts. They assume responsibility for organization, facilitation, and the passing of the baton for their two meetings. The experience and objectification stages of each meeting require the formation of two groups of five participants (including one peer facilitator) in two rooms, each of which contains video equipment. One participant should bring her or his own daycare center's video recorder to make this distribution possible. These groups of five will remain constant in their composition through the whole process of the study group, and both must be represented in the choice of peer facilitators.

Table 4
An example of an integrated video study group

Sharing responsibilities in the video study group

Once the participants and the peer facilitator, after obtaining advice from their mentor, have settled upon a theme, the discourse types to be practiced, how these will be rotated, and perhaps other aspects of the professional competency, their program is ripe for action. What remains to be organized is cooperation among the participants.

The tasks to be shared will be chosen in common, using a list of propositions made by the mentor or following principles of cooperation. These tasks situate the group within shared learning. ("Shared learning" is an instructional concept integrating strategies of cooperative learning [Cohen 1994a, 1994b; Kagan 1992; Johnson and Johnson 1994] and reciprocal learning [Rosenshine and Meister 1994].) They can be in line with those specified by a practicum guide, drawn up like maps, or written as a scenario. A scenario indicates a module's components to participants as possible trajectories for getting the process of education or change launched.

Cooperative groups are self-managed, using precise operational instructions or tasks. For example, the scenario could describe the rotation of tasks among learners (see Figure 3).

For instance, for a group of sixteen learners, the scenario would describe interactions to be organized: 1) among learners M_1-N_1-O_1-

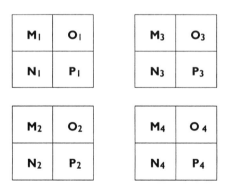

Figure 3
Distribution of sixteen learners in four groups

P_1; then 2) between reciprocal learners M_1-O_1 and N_1-P_1; 3) between learners N_1-O_1 and M_1-P_1 following an individual practice session; 4) among cooperative learners M_1-M_2-M_3-M_4; between M_1 and N_2; and so on. This session design allows for combining educational strategies with the distribution of discourse types and themes among workshops. Video feedback could relate to these rotation strategies. Such feedback could be organized as roundtable discussions, using the same rotational principle as critical confrontations, following screenings of the videotapes. The distribution of tasks proposed by a shared scenario could relate to a half-day meeting, but it can also be spread out over time and relate to practices lasting several months.

Don't think that content is being neglected, or that you are denying the importance of educational excellence as regards both subject matter and the practical transfer necessary to work within a given discipline. A pedagogical video study group can be transformed into a pedagogical workshop in order to address the organization of relations in terms of the disciplinary knowledge conveyed. What precedes can be applied to the creation of disciplinary video study groups as well.

Choosing a reflection paradigm
for the video study group

Reflective analysis can unfold in three stages. (Note: What follows is inspired by Lefebvre and Poncet-Montange [1996].)

1. Segmentation of the phases of the professional act, and then of the sense units, right down to the smallest.

2. Identification of observable elements of interaction: what is said, done, and shown by the professional, or by interlocutors, is noted on an observation grid. These elements are classified using a communications diagram, as are methods and the modes and functions of the speech act.

3. Interpretive reading of the video data: possible intersection of analytical grids derived from item 2; place-

ment in relation to the theoretical model, using a series of questions; development of heuristics.

In an education-research team working in the field of daycare, daycare teachers are conducting reflective analysis based on a model for development of thought and action (Gravel, Parent, and Tremblay 1995; Palkiewicz 1990). This model defines four levels of thought:

- The empirical level (intake of sensory data)
- The conceptual level (placement of data in relation to prior data)
- The rational level (transformation of data through reasoning and logical operations)
- The decision-making level (integration of the data into plans for action and decision making)

A fifth level of thought is constituted by reflection properly so called (metacognition) and applied to the first four levels. This leads the individual to consider four forms of awareness of mental operations. The analysis of personal narratives and verbal reflections by students in daycare techniques allows one to follow their growth toward reflective professionalism.

In the experiment conducted in Guinea that was described to illustrate the individualized video study group, reflective growth was analyzed using a model that reduces the process of reflection to four cyclical stages:

- Attention to concrete and personal experience
- Examination, analysis, and identification of key factors and models
- Formulation of concepts, rules, and principles
- Development of a personal theory tested in a new situation (Holborn 1992, 85-103)

The mentor elicited the student teacher's attention to the unfolding of this process by identifying these four stages in the student teacher's discourse for each of the targeted competencies.

The competencies were written up as scripts and then reflected upon along various dimensions. These questions raise the learners' level of self-examination and incite them to produce better models of their own action and, as a consequence, to improve their action.

The important thing is to choose a procedure that is consistent with the frame of discussion within which one is working, as Chapter Three will show.

In Brief

It's not possible to make simultaneous use of all the elements described in this chapter on organizing interactions in the educational video study group. While some (like the cooperation scenario and the organization of sessions according to a discursive orientation) can be used concurrently or sequentially, nevertheless a choice must be made as to which options are preferred. A mentor or facilitator who, while reading this book, notes those elements that appear most likely to suit her or his own context will end up with a set of practical suggestions allowing for the design of study group meetings suited to the clientele. But these suggestions will have to be negotiated step by step. By tying together those elements of the planned and negotiated program that can be worked upon jointly as part of a shared theme or a group activity, one improves the potential for organizing a coherent and motivating experience.

A few ways of organizing various video-pedagogy situations have been brought together here, but it is not desirable to be dogmatic on the subject. More than one approach is valid, and whatever approach is adopted, every group will find that it must shape the model in question to suit its own context.

Indicate below the method of organization for your video study group's meetings:

A TAILORED VIDEO STUDY GROUP	+
Projects	
Targeted competencies	
Themes addressed	
Number of participants	
Number of meetings	
Shared organization	
Process for deepening knowledge	
Work on discourse	
Interaction effects	
Process of reflection	

CHAPTER THREE

Choosing a Frame for Discussion

Video pedagogy is above all a new method of growth. It defines the methods of interaction and feedback through dialogue in encounters for reflective practice; and the essential instrument of its implementation is feedback on practice. Interactions are videotaped and then screened and conceptualized with the goal of the common creation of new knowledge. This knowledge can contribute to change in the work setting.

For instance, teachers in an elementary school decided to combine several grades for certain activities. Curriculum changes were then made through joint action, with the video study group providing a regulatory process. Cooperation among teachers led to a modification in habits and customs. Thus, learning and change are defined through the creation of hitherto unknown knowledge, using a frame for interaction that includes the tasks involved and retroactive discussion.

A video study group provides a flexible coming together of a network of people involved in research, with the goal of education, professional development, or change. It is not enough to organize interactions: it is necessary to *go back over* those interactions, to engage in feedback. The effects of video feedback — though anxiety-provoking — are fundamental for social competency education (Saunders and Hargie 1989). Their impact is so great that video feedback is increasingly being used in various professional and educational settings, including special education (Hansen and Mounty 1995). Hence the importance of specifying a *frame for the discussion* — of what principles underlie the retrospective formulation of opinions and the nature of its purpose.

The frame for discussion specifies the point of impact of feedback. The way video is used is closely dependent on the frame for discussion chosen by the cooperative group. It must be concerted and well defined. Every study group has its own frame of reference. That is why, without any claim to exhaustiveness, several frames for discussion are presented here that allow for an adjustment of the meetings to suit the needs of participants from specific communities. (A more complete list can be found in Bertrand [1995] and in Denzin and Lincoln [1994]. An exhaustive presentation of curriculum trends is proposed in Pinard, Reynolds, Slattery, and Taubman [1995].)

In education, the following frames have been found to be especially useful:

1. The *functional frame* is aimed at activity mastery and orients activities according to the results of the task to be performed. The discussion is organized around well-defined objectives and deals with effective behavior and with performance.

2. The *psychocognitive strategic frame* emphasizes the conceptual structures of learning. In this case, discussion bears on plan actualization, interactive decisions, cognitive styles, work methods, and the mental strategies employed in problem solving.

3. The *sociocognitive constructivist frame* links the process of coming to awareness with authentic experiences that challenge widely held notions. The culture of cooperative learning that is thus created brings about epistemic conflicts and models situations by analogy.

4. The *sociocritical frame* functions within a social, democratic, and participative perspective, and proposes empowerment over the act of learning and examination of

those aspects of interaction that turn education into a process of either oppression or liberation. The approach can be feminist, ethnic, ethical, ecological, social, and so on.

5. The *personal frame* is the foundation for autobiographical or narrative approaches to human experience. It is focused on the individual. The process of personal growth is linked to a humanist, phenomenological, psychoanalytical, or spiritual approach to experience.

6. The *pragmatic frame* is focused on the language of practice. The explicitation of practical arguments and of the intentions related to situations allows for an exploration of knowledge in its context. Conversations about the grounds for action link know-how to knowledge.

The role of theory is changing in education; from being prescriptive, it is tending toward a descriptive role. Its goal is dialogue and reflection. It removes contingency from the arena in order to highlight significant elements. Through a double motion, it then entails return to the concrete. Passage from the general to the particular indicates the context within which theorized practice may be reinvested.

Every theory corresponds to a community of research, reflection, and discussion. A video study group's discussion workshops create in little what is found writ large in the scholarly world. They establish consensus on incipient new knowledge. They constitute small academies, and their playful dimension facilitates access to them. The study group's human dimension allows for an emphasis on friendship as part of the process of professionalization and injects a motivating component for participants. Study groups for professional discussion offer new perspectives on action. Video tends to focus discussion on concrete phenomena and practical interaction.

The pluralism of ways of seeing is inspired by a democratic vision of teaching. Many examples of this are provided here. The nature of the interactions will differ according to the theoretical frame adopted.

Before an educational video study group is launched, it is important to know what frame is desired for reflection. Every frame will have specific implications for the organization of meetings. The frames for discussion presented here are currently high-profile in education; they have had a certain impact within many countries. You will find presented here ways of integrating them into the process of education, professional development, and change in teaching.

The Functional Video Study Group

The *functional frame* centers discussion on effectiveness and performance. Here the educational goal is to train learners to engage in interaction in a progressive and simple way, with video feedback being used for the purpose. Thus, video recording fills the gap between practice and theory, and their being brought closer together is what makes it possible to function.

The term *function* designates any correspondence between two classes of objects. For example, it could indicate the gestures needed to achieve a goal. Functions refer to coordinated operations that ensure goals are achieved and activities maintained. Functional models preserve a harmonious balance in performance by discriminating criteria for perfection. Adjustment to the task setting is then based on criteria for effectiveness.

The functional frame presupposes that for every criterion that indicates successful adjustment to the setting, it is possible to identify particular predictors. The postulate, then, is that operating these predictors will increase functional effectiveness. In this perspective, one seeks to identify behaviors (predictors) that are highly correlated with success. Behaviors that constitute good predictors of the desired performance are progressively integrated into the educational process (Berliner 1989, 3-22; Brophy and Good 1986, 328-376; Carroll 1989; Kulik, Kulik, and Bangert-Drowns 1990).

Thus, it's a question of discovering behaviors that facilitate students' success and then working on these behaviors, because they are identified with correspondence between two sets of objects, namely:

1. Behaviors observable through video feedback

2. Final performance, as defined using criteria that are equally subject to observation

The perspective taken is that of organizing complex activities focused on a desired result. It consists of comparing participants' behaviors with set objectives. For example:

- The performance that is to be worked on in common is presented on video. It is analyzed and understood in all its complexity. Criteria for good performance are developed in common.

- Participants plan performance together; they establish choices by referring to the previously analyzed models. They differentiate significant sequences within the body of the overall performance.

- Participants practice those sequences in order to progressively arrive at the desired performance. The order of the sequences is not really important; what is important is to reconstitute a presentation that is significant in relation to the overall performance. Work on detail is conducted with an eye to the whole.

- Performance sequences are screened, with the mentor, before individuals, peers, or the group. Participants develop an acute critical understanding of the criteria for a successful performance.

- Sequences, and eventually the whole performance, are gone over in an ever broader setting.

- At every stage, progress in performance is evaluated.

This vision of education allows one to see behavior in a holistic perspective, with a grasp of broad individual units that can be used as modules appropriate to the context of action. The functional paradigm will allow for the creation of original video study groups, if individuals are prepared to free themselves up from the structures presented in microeducational units. It is only thus that functioning can be envisioned within comprehensive projects.

The point is to privilege functional relations among actors within a project. In this spirit, many behaviors may be considered acceptable, so long as they bring about the desired objective. Functional diagnostic methods are put into place, with their focal point being the purpose of the action. Thus, feedback optimizes the functional elements operating in the video study group.

Let's look at an example.

Example 1: Integrating the functional frame

Salomé teaches theater arts in a conservatory. Every year, with her colleague Deborah, who teaches singing, she carries out a major project. This year, they have chosen an abridged version of Bizet's *Carmen*. They have brought together the dance and singing classes to view two film adaptations of *Carmen* on video. (Note: To present movies on video to an audience of learners, you must receive permission for educational broadcast.)

Deborah explains the progress of the opera and the stages in which the scenes the students are to act will be mounted. She and Salomé demonstrate the gestures and movements it will be necessary to work on. With the students, they repeatedly screen the cigar factory battle scene and the tavern scene. The choreography for the two scenes is then devised.

For three months, singing and dance are rehearsed separately on Saturdays, dance in the morning and singing in the afternoon, and teaching is based on video feedback, objectification, and reinvestment within an ever broader context. Eventually, voice and movement are combined; and to all of this, set and costumes are added.

In the morning, Salomé works with the class on theatrical and choreographic aspects. Videotaping the class motivates the students; it represents a significant method of self-correction. After all, Salomé can't see everything or explain everything. She hasn't got the time to attend to each individual. The students, on the other hand, have reached a stage where they can spot errors and correct each other. A leg is badly placed, the turn-out is not quite right.

Sequences are reviewed as work progresses. For this purpose, Salomé puts her Hi-8 camcorder in remote mode. Two cords link the camcorder to an ordinary TV screen whose remote control has been set to AV. Screening doesn't take long. She doesn't erase sequences; rather she records them continuously so that students can review them later. This way they memorize them better. Sequences are practiced immediately, with an effort to correct bearing. For example, Patricia checks the height of her arm in order to ensure it matches the group.

The singing class is conducted in the afternoon as a master class, with guest instructors. The five soloists rehearse under the direction of the masters. Those singing the parts of officers and gypsies attend and then together work on the choral components. Video feedback relates to interpretive exercises and overall bearing during performance. For instance, is it tense? Is the mouth properly shaped or not? In auditory and visual terms, much emerges from the videotape: quality of sound, gestures and their meaning (or their failure to support the meaning of the libretto).

Performances are taped on Saturdays, and the students may rescreen these tapings and discuss them in small groups in the screening room, as they desire. A large-group feedback session is arranged every Wednesday afternoon. As the weeks go by, Salomé and Deborah start to bring their two classes together. During feedback, they come to stress the look. For instance, during one trio including a pas-de-deux, the students are not unified. They are failing to make eye contact. They work on this component as part of the singing and the choreography.

The videotape contributes a great deal: sometimes things go by fast, and only a screening allows for a full awareness of detail and improvement of performance.

Functional operation

As the preparation of this theatrical presentation unfolds, trajectories emerge within which the group cooperates for a common mastery of technique. Certain cases are chosen to show which actions are or are not in harmony with the desired performance. Both teachers and participants work through several successive phases. Can you identify them? (If you find yourself hesitating, consult Chapter Two.)

Look at your own program of study in the perspective of a comprehensive project. Organize a set of activities with a functional orientation, using video feedback to achieve progress. How would you do this? How would you share experiences? How would you articulate the process of self-questioning?

Functional practice

▼ You and a colleague are working together to prepare a video workshop for the development of "expert learners." You determine a general objective that represents a comprehensive project.

Project

▼ Consider this general objective to be the outcome of your sequence and apply the rule of the necessary preliminaries: What is the sequence of objectives and criteria that will lead to the unfolding of this project? Find at least five intermediate objectives.

1.

2.

3.

4.

5.

▼ If you have identified five intermediate objectives that will function to help your project unfold, this means that you have correctly fulfilled your task. Now add criteria for success.

1a.

2a.

3a.

4a.

5a.

▼ Reread your criteria and apply them to yourself. Have you met them? If not, it's probably because they are too demanding. Adjust your criteria. What will you teach your learners so that they develop these objectives? Rearticulate these objectives within a project and write out a list of indispensable contents. Look at these contents again in light of the objectives. Do you think it will be possible to handle them in the time available?

Relate the objectives to the workshop activities: What shoots will be used? What use will be made of the screening and of video feedback? When you meet with your "expert learners" let the most agitated member of the group handle the camcorder; this has a calming effect.

Your objective is to improve. Collect the shoots of key learning moments. Spend one evening a week looking over the best sequences with the person who is giving you technical assistance. Determine your criteria and focus on performance.

▼ Don't forget: You are reflecting within a functional frame. You are teaching learners to reflect on their own objectives, stage by stage: reflection before action, reflection in action, reflection following action. You develop your techniques for self-questioning "before," "during," and "after." Techniques are then reinvested in the video study group, and there is peer evaluation using a question card.

For example:

1. Is the subject matter pitched to knowledge and problems that suit your interlocutors' levels?

2. Is the subject matter easily understood, and is it clearly presented?

3. Are the components of optimal functioning clearly set out?

4. Are the hypotheses and solutions logical?

5. Are the stages of task fulfillment clearly explained?

In the following section, we will see how the functional perspective has been broadened to become a concept centered on cognitive strategies that facilitate problem solving.

The Strategic Video Study Group

Underlying each performance is a competency for which the performance is the indicator. The goal of education is to develop the competency that enactment manifests. Performance is a product of knowledge. If education is centered on competency, discussion must be oriented toward the delicate creation of the conditions for the competencies necessary in problem solving.

The word *strategy* designates a process that allows you to get past a problem-space. You identify simple strategies (algorithms) and complex strategies (heuristics) that can be used for complex situations. (See Schoenfeld [1985] for a helpful presentation of the components of problem solving.) The teacher, mentor, or peer facilitator explicates strategies by contextualizing the conditions of their implementation. She or he addresses the organization of contents as well as the strategies implemented to fulfill the task to be learned. Participants in the video study group analyze clinical problems and engage in exchange on concrete events. (Note: "Clinical analysis" refers to observation of empirical phenomena. It is based on data rather than on a pre-existing theory.) Self-teaching is valued, and communication becomes important in overcoming concrete obstacles.

In this context, the video study group is designed as a whole, organized for the development of problem-solving strategies. Group problem solving entails several phases. For example:

- Jointly defining the problem's variables by specifying "if ... then" conditions of action.

- Mapping these causal chains (this can be done in graphic form).

- Planning a goal that tends toward the solution of the problem analyzed; reaching small-group agreement on the phases of achievement of the negotiated and selected goal.

- Carrying out these phases in view of resolving the problem analyzed; verifying the goal and evaluating the activities.

Analysis is the main approach used to acquire and integrate educational concepts. Types of knowledge are given a significant role in information processing. *Declarative* knowledge corresponds to the "what" and pins down factual data; it is static and must be transformed into procedure to lead to action. *Procedural* knowledge corresponds to the "how"; it is dynamic and indicates procedures for action. Procedural sequences correspond to sequences of action and not to high-level category rules for evaluating the context and specific conditions for action within a concrete situation. The latter is the role of *contextual* or *conditional* knowledge, which determines the "when" and the "why" of a strategy's implementation, while evaluating process (Jones 1990; Marzano *et al.* 1988; Sternberg and Horvath 1995). In a strategic workshop, problem solving is analyzed in terms of conditions of action. (*If* condition A is encountered, *then* condition B must be envisioned.)

Various situations may be subject to specific conditions for action. The peer facilitator invites participants to take account of this by remaining attentive to it during the course of action. This approach, which is used not only in the education of teachers but also of technicians, nurses, and physicians, has the advantage of familiarizing participants in teamwork with the ethical implications of decision making. The inductive discovery phase, which is centered on problems, is complemented by a deductive final approach.

For example, a group will strive together to determine the conditions for optimal action. Then they will specify the deductive conditions of action. For instance:

> Luke is a member of a strategic video study group of young orchestra conductors. He identifies the various strategies he uses when he observes that certain instruments are not in tune:
>
> - IF a rehearsal is under way, THEN he interrupts everything until the instrumentalists have tuned up.
>
> - IF this is a dress rehearsal, THEN he suggests a break for tuning at the end of a musical sequence.
>
> - IF a concert is in progress, THEN he points to the instrumentalist with his baton so that that person can

tune the instrument as soon as an opportunity presents itself.

Luke was not even aware of his own strategic gradation.
It became clear to him through the process of reflection
on practice that the video allowed for; and indeed, the
other learners discovered their own.

During the last two decades, research on cognitive strategies has
produced important results that have been experimentally validated
(Rosenshine 1997, p. 6):

1. It allows for the teaching of "fuzzy know-how" — that
   is, knowledge that is tacit and for which each step
   cannot be made explicit.

2. Prompts were developed in various domains to scaffold
   learning and teach heuristics.

3. The procedures used by experts were elicited and used
   for enhancing the competencies of novices.

4. Instructional programs were developed using thinking
   aloud, cue cards, and checklists to anticipate students'
   errors and help them concretely use heuristic prompts.

The video study group allows for the construction of strategic
knowledge.

Video allows us to root knowledge in a reality that is both
experiential and objectifiable. It makes possible critical comparison
among personal experiences and among interpersonal experiences.
It makes us partners in cognition (Solomon, Perkins, and Globerson
1991). In this way, it fosters postures of research; the formulation of
hypotheses; and experimentation, verification, and evaluation of
acts and their consequences, through movement back and forth
between knowledge and deeds, each regulating the other. Through
the establishment of a close relationship between action and professional concepts, experiences take root and become routine.

In this perspective, the video study group assigns an important
role to motivation and to strategies that consist of learning how to
learn. Emphasis is placed on the broadening of knowledge and on

one's capacity to make links between the contents and interactors' prior knowledge. The mentor shows participants how to organize interactions within problem-solving contexts and how to act as a motivating mediator between knowledge and the interactor.

Example 2: Integrating the strategic frame

The first video study group I ever tried operated over two semesters and included seven to nine video recordings, each one followed by a discussion group session for screening and lightly directed formative evaluation on shoots taken the previous week. This experience occurred as part of a teacher education program. The student teachers' guide included ten useful competencies for pedagogical interaction:

Teacher-centered Competencies:

- Well-planned improvisation
- Individualizing experience
- Use of the professional semiotic system (gestures, images, sound, light)
- Variation in interactive styles
- Scripting information

Learner-centered Competencies:

- Detecting and adjusting to the interlocutor's mode of access to information
- Eliciting reflection on social goals and on individual predispositions in order to motivate
- Cooperating
- Listening
- Negotiating

Each participant would choose the competency she or he wished to develop. The first recordings were made in studio and then in a school setting. The student teachers went through a period of professional practice in November-December. Those who have already experienced the job setting find that a simulated setting takes little account of the contextual realities of the workplace.

WALTER: "During my practice teaching, I learned that you can't study up on interaction. You learn about it on the job. It was a difficult, sometimes demoralizing learning process."

For this reason, the organization of what eventually became a video study group was adjusted each year to respond to problems and suggestions raised by the student teachers. The first year, three observations were made in January:

1. In order to enhance the value of the video recordings, it was necessary to prolong them. A longer recording time allowed for the exercise of negotiating skills and certain complex competencies.

2. This meant, however, that participants had to make a selection of relevant clips before screening sessions.

3. After an initial experimental phase, it was necessary to work on "abnormal" problem situations — those that constitute real professional pitfalls rather than re-duced-complexity situations.

Sessions were progressively lengthened, depending on the group (the study group consisted of three workshops of eight participants each). We worked on stretches of twenty to thirty minutes of recording or on continuous recording of the whole group, with each person permitted to intervene to show how she or he would resolve a problematic situation. Two tools were used in parallel with the screening of experiences: participants organized their experiences using concept maps, and they kept a log.

The following year, we planned for post-practicum perceptions. We negotiated flexible modules of variable duration, depending on need. This held for screenings and feedback sessions as well. We planned four screenings on practicums (other screenings sub-sequently took place according to individual initiative). Generally, practicum tapings related to each person's best fifteen to twenty minutes of recording — those that seemed the most typical of a problem encountered in the field.

We took into account the need for in-depth reflection on complex settings. A consensus was established that each student teacher should be videotaped in class in a school setting during her or his practicum. The program was carefully adapted to the educational needs of each team. The fundamental aspects of interaction served as conceptual tools for reflection on lived experience and made possible the communication of experience. Thus, the video study group operated in a state of ongoing exploration.

Following our initial experiences, we increased the number of self- and other-viewing sessions by arranging for several tailored meetings in order to meet the need for individualized and better-situated learning in small groups. The rhythm of the sessions needed to be adapted to new experiences in the school setting. The transition from video study group to professional setting was made by integrating video recording into school activities. Little by little, we added intermediate phases of the screening of experience videotaped by peers, so that only those issues on which conceptual work had already been done by the group were brought back to the group. As well, recording rhythm had to be adapted to participants' capacities. Depending on their work setting, they went through periods of overload that had to be taken into account.

Here is a second example of integration of the strategic frame. At the end of Chapter Two, we looked at reflective analysis by an education-research team studying daycare techniques. This team identified nine fundamental competencies for a teacher in an early-childhood care center:

1. Improvisation

2. Organization of the surroundings

3. Interaction management

4. Individualization of one's approach

5. Stimulation

6. Communication with the child

7. Communication with coworkers

8. Curriculum management

10. Demonstration of professionalism.

A set of abilities was specified for each competency and associated with a series of possible role plays of various real-life professional situations. This educational program is based on a cycle of videotaped experience, individual peer analysis, the writing of a personal narrative, and a group screening of videotapes in order to reflect on the competencies developed.

Strategic operation

The process described above can serve as the basis for organizing meetings that would help intervenors lead their interactors in developing professional competency. Invite them to reflect on their last activity, with a video recording as a point of departure. Make use of a narrative of experience. Have them tell each other their perception of events. Were there moments of strength or passive moments? Did they change their plans? Why? What was their spontaneous strategic gradation (an unforeseen gradation)? What were their conditions for action? How did they help interactors take on their share of the decision-making process, using available resources? What contents could people choose?

In this way, you can open the study group's first sessions by situating yourself in a problem-solving context.

Strategic practice

What a mentor can organize for participants in a video study group, education professionals can do amongst themselves. For example, if you wish to progress and to deepen your strategies, you can do the following:

▼ Find two coworkers who are interested in trying out a strategic experiment.

Together, plan a module focused on the integration of a competency that is well contextualized within your discipline or field work. Record some aspects of its implementation and then confront your own experiences. Each person should present a report. Together, develop a key-concept map of your reports, link the concepts with arrows, and compare their conceptual structure while justifying ᵥ choices made.

▼ Organize a strategy group.

Comment on the scenario you plan to use for interaction. Each participant will tape her or his implementations and then bring them back to the video study group for examination. Meetings will consist of comments on the clips each person brings for group discussion. Record the progress of group discussion in the form of brief surveys, by asking participants to summarize a given phase of their progress. Then, ask certain participants about their own methods of work. Replay the video recording at the end of the module and compare participant methods.

▼ Confront your experiences.

Among you, apply a video study group strategy. Reflective strategies allow you to work on a "meta" level: you will be working on other participants' work and at the same time on your own.

The most highly developed and context-sensitive strategic approaches within cognitivism are in harmony with a constructivist frame for discussion, as we discuss next.

The Constructivist Video Study Group

As distinguished from the strategic video study group, which works on problem solving by defining optimal conditions for action, the constructivist study group is based on situational models. Discussion relates to the co-construction of knowledge within a community whose significations are the subject of exchange.

In this interpretive framework, meaning-making processes are shared in communities of learners. Knowledge comes from belonging to — and engaging in communication with — a specific cultural community (Davydov 1995; DeVries 1997; Driver, Asoko, Leach, Mortimer, and Scott 1994). The video study group, then, constitutes one of the loci of exchange and of validation of knowledge.

Within this frame, it may no longer be adequate to speak of "teaching" or "training." Education is not conceived of independently of those educated. At the very most, one can talk of a pedagogy of sharing, cooperative in nature. Adjustment to situations allows for a gradual development of balanced action. Thus, the video study group constitutes a *modus vivendi* for cooperative self-development. Because it reveals identity in action, the constructivist study group can become an integrated approach to identity formation (Penuel and Wertsch 1995).

The claim that identity is socially constructed accommodates the further claim that actions are grounded in situations. Therefore, one should learn in complex, social settings. Though these claims should not be overstated (Anderson, Reder, and Simon 1996), they explain why the orientation of the constructivist video study group is toward modeling and reflecting on cases and situations. Discussion is situated; it is attuned not only to the regular rhythms of professional action, to typical similarities, but also to the exception, to unique trajectories, to sudden events, to the impromptu. In professional education, a constructivist approach addresses unexpected events and behaviors; unforeseen or difficult cases are envisaged; and critical incidents are worked on. In adult education, one would attune oneself to unstable situations requiring a reframing that breaks with the universe of beliefs inherited from logical rationalism. In these circumstances, the video study group becomes the tool for adjusting the process of change.

Using these presuppositions, educational action operates on a communication contract specifying the model of action that will flow from the knowledge to be constructed. This contract will be articulated so that:

- A constructive role is assigned to the participant — that is, the participant takes responsibility for her or his own development, along with the peer facilitator.

- Higher education is given a social dimension, and this dimension is contextualized through work on credible and complex professional situations.

Since professional practice is interactive, interaction becomes the unit of analysis. Current constructivist theories redefine the concept of knowledge; they follow the postmodern trend in attempting to reconceptualize the way we view epistemology (Green

1994, 423-464; Woods and Murphy 1997). The definition of knowledge as shared conceptualization commits intervenors to a radical break with top-down conceptions of education, according to which truth or several truths must be imparted to the learners (von Glaserfeld 1995). Meaning is constantly subjected to interpretation and negotiation. In this way, video pedagogy becomes based on interactionism. It handles the reality seen on tape with questions such as: How do social, cultural, and historical conditions constitute the process by which students learn to act professionally or by which active professionals achieve further development? (Vare 1993, p. 1).

Within this frame of reference, analysis of the process involved in the professional act leads to specifying the nature of the interaction. What historic factors influenced its development? What are the cultural products used and conceived of within the workshop? In what way does the video study group's situation imbue certain cultural behaviors with validity?

The peer facilitator must work within the learners' developmental zone by assessing their capacity for cognitive conflict in the progression in which they hope to engage. This optimal developmental zone, collaboratively built, is situated at the crossroads of the individual and social worlds, and it must be negotiated by relatively seasoned actors.

Example 3: Integrating the constructivist frame

Peder (Note: Peder died some months ago, and this passage is homage to his dedication and generosity as a teacher) taught management, administration, and accounting in a junior and community college. He was fascinated with the constructivist perspective. He saw that optimal learning can only be accomplished within a group, with students coming together to develop knowledge that is useful in the execution of projects.

In order to better understand the functioning of groups of learners, Peder asked permission to record students on video. The video documents were used as a complement to their class work and were the basis not for individual, but for group evaluation. At the same time, they allowed Peder to share his cooperative experiences with his colleagues.

As department head, Peder was responsible for curriculum reform. To his colleagues, he suggested monthly meetings for exchange on experiences videotaped in class.

Peder gave each person a degree of responsibility. In this way, he
helped his colleagues as well as his students develop positive interdependence: they became resources for each other. His teaching was
centered on cohesiveness within heterogeneous learning groups,
each of which comprised a balanced representation of strong and
weak members for each field discussed. Thus, he invited his students to work simultaneously on two levels:

- They were to create a group culture favorable to
  learning, which required the use of cooperative competencies.

- They assumed responsibility for achieving the goals
  that the group set for itself, according to a semi-for-
  mal contract with the teacher.

The problem Peder resolved using video is the following: most
research on cooperative learning recommends individual, summative evaluation based on the criterion grid accompanying the instructional contract. Peder managed to develop a group criterion-based
evaluation. He introduced his colleagues to this approach and helped
them develop a culture of shared learning within their own classrooms.

Constructivist operation

1. Develop an observation grid using cooperative criteria
   for evaluating the group learning process. Design it so
   that evaluation is delegated to one member of the
   group. Suggest to the group's participants that they
   videotape themselves in order to assess the level of
   reciprocity in their cooperation.

2. Develop a summative grid allowing for evaluation of a
   dossier or project created by a whole group, and of the
   constructive interdependence of participants in the
   fulfillment of the task. Use video clips of the group to

better integrate criteria in the form of sociocognitive rules. Name individuals who will be responsible for each criterion.

Constructivist practice

▼ Distribute your students in heterogeneous groups, using criteria allowing you to build positive interdependence within each group; for example: distribution of different levels within each group (one strong member, one weak member, two average members); distribution of learning styles (one rationalist member, one intuitive member, and one empirical member in each group). Then suggest that they become experts on dossiers and engage in mutual education. They can produce a videotaped report. Videotape the group's activities and, with their permission, bring the tapes to an evening session among mentors, teachers, or facilitators, for discussion and for exchange about pedagogical ideas. This actually constitutes the beginnings of a video study group.

The constructivist approach allows for the adoption of a more nuanced position in analyzing situations than that of a classic problem-solving approach. Most strategic authors dissociate cognitive tools from their context and treat them as mental objects, as though they had a concrete existence. A radical and constructivist orientation, like its extension, the sociocritical orientation, suggests, on the contrary, that such methods of categorization are and remain socially constructed interpretations, whose sharing and comprehension are based on tacitly understood assumptions and shared subjectivity (Phillips 1995).

In the constructivist perspective, strategy is defined as the way a power and knowledge relationship based on a particular culture is constituted through a process of negotiation. It subsequently helps those who participated in this negotiation to build the power and knowledge connections that result from it (Vare 1993, p. 3).

On this basis, certain new-wave, "liberated" video study groups based on social criticism have been developed, as described below.

The Sociocritical Video Study Group

An educational video study group can be designed on a sociocritical basis. In this instance, video pedagogy is based on methods for emancipating participants and their interactors. It is centered on the social construction of identity and on empowerment. To the extent that the sociocritical approach is opposed to an elitist conception of professionalization and education, because these reproduce social inequalities, sociocritical pedagogy will focus on the discovery of modes of influence within relationships and on empowerment of participants for their own learning (Freire 1997; Apple 1990; Latour 1997; McLaren 1991; Giroux 1992). Participants in a sociocritical video study group work to unveil the process of social stratification. To accomplish this, peer facilitators can, for instance, suggest to participants in their groups a logic of actualization based on four complementary thrusts:

- *Thematic contextualization* — the theme must interest participants and relate to their experience.

- *Critical problematization* — the theme deals with a problem faced by participants that requires change.

- *Awareness raising* — both the individual and the group come to see themselves as subjects, and they plan change.

- *Manifestation* — change comes about through individual or collective initiative and in line with plans (Pruyn 1993).

This process is related to the project-based process.

The video study group leads participants to deconstruct professional language games. Video allows for the movement back and forth from being to seeming, and to the words with which we dress up experience — and work comes to take on a playful dimension. Learning and play merge in the video study group. By examining the *raison d'être* of the cultural roles assumed by the different partners, deconstruction brings to light the knowledge and power connections inherent in a workshop, defined by knowledge issues and arising out of the historical context of the program for education, professional development, or change.

Sociocritical pedagogy prevents the video study group from degenerating into a series of prescriptive and incapacitating rules for participants. It incites a denunciation of ways of making attitudes homogeneous. It can highlight cultural difference and, through simulated practice, reveal social norms that reinforce dominant stereotypes while repressing individuals' autonomous achievement.

Interpretation of social experience and a reading of cultural patterns orients critique and reveals the biases that lead us, for example, to see the role of the intervenor as that of someone who does not get involved in other people's affective life. Critical analysis could demonstrate the intervenor's social nature and the potential for oppression in the imposed convention of distance. For example, by defining the intervenor as a friend whose relational function is to care for the other's development and to look out for it, feminist critique shows the affective and transformative impact of interaction professions. (Note: There are historic roots for this point of view. Aristotle described education as a moral form of friendship. See Fenstermacher [1990, 130-154].) This impact is conveyed by means of "nonverbal meta-lessons" (Flinders 1991, 15) rather than through a technical dissection of behavioral units.

Example 4: Integrating the sociocritical frame

Barbara is a social worker in a recreational center in the suburb of a big city. She has started up a video study group with a group of hackers. Hackers are young people whose main occupation is to crack protected computer data; they take pride in using their ingenuity to pirate data banks and to create computer viruses that sabotage the operation of recent software. In Barbara's view, a critical exchange of social reflections might lead them to change their perspective, and so she has opted for a sociocritical orientation.

In suggesting to these young people that they recount their experiences at weekly meetings, her goal is to offer them an opportunity to reflect upon their actions. Pulling back to reflect might lead them to adopt a more democratic social attitude. Accompanying

Barbara down this road is a team of professionals brought together as part of a reflective Balint group: each intervenor reports on her or his own experiences and tries to work out what is implicit in them through different testimonials.

Not much is known about these meetings, because participants are bound to secrecy, but two evenings spent with the young hackers have had an impact on discussions held in the group. The question asked was whether something negative can be reinvested to positive effect.

Barbara learns that the members of her small group of hackers have each been working on the issue independently. They have been visiting "mind-blowing" sites on the Internet, which elicit from them harsh reactions leading to awareness raising. The videotaped moments speak eloquently. Barbara gets the young people to discuss the matter. They have tracked down fascist sites and are shaken by what they see. Suddenly they understand the word *war*, and they contextualize the violence they experience at school (Devine 1996). They start to take cognizance of history, of the meaning of words, and of arms. Since they spend their days programming anti-programs, they get launched on a discussion of the following question: "Why try to destroy commercial software that provides people with jobs and lets them put food on the table?"

The video study group leads them to pool their efforts. They confront their own experiences and phone each other to talk about their discoveries.

The group takes on a project: to destroy a fascist site on the Internet. Barbara tries to get them to reflect on fundamentalisms and principled rigidity of all kinds, but their project has taken root. Because they can't insinuate a virus into a text file, they design a program for the exponential replication of e-mail. One of the young people succeeds in hacking a server through overload.

Barbara now comes to her Balint group sessions bearing the traces of her hackers' activism. For three sessions, the group has been stuck on the question of good and evil. During this time, a fascist organization has penetrated a university's mainframe. At the last meeting of the video study group, the young hackers held a council on whether it was ethically necessary and physically possible to cause the breakdown of the central server for this university.

Sociocritical operation

Identify what is troubling in Barbara's role. Are educational practices of this kind acceptable? Think of similar cases in your own discipline or profession in which you sometimes adopt a morally unclear attitude. From what point of view does the moral unclarity exist? What would a democratic attitude consist of? Engage in a discussion on these cases. Adopt a sociocritical perspective. Does this perspective lead to a project? How could video feedback be integrated into it?

Sociocritical practice

▼ You are a mentor of educators. Every week, they present personal accounts of serious cases they deal with in their work setting. How would you plan your sessions to allow these educators-in-training to free themselves from the doctrinal limitations their own education has so far imposed on them? How could you help them deal with their experiences from a critical perspective?

▼ You are a teacher, and the beginning of the school year was marked by problems connected to the appalling relationships among several of the students. Sometimes it seems to you the class is beyond your control. Two coworkers close to you share this view. You'd like a better understanding of whether your own attitude is influencing the students' behavior, and you'd like to better grasp the social dynamics of this class. Video feedback could help you. How would you go about it?

▼ You work in higher education. You observe that there are walls between disciplines and between faculties that to some extent prohibit communication among professors. So you invite over an interdisciplinary group including diverse faculty members. How will you help them surmount these cultural barriers and adopt a critical attitude toward the stereotypes associated with these barriers? How could video contribute to an opening up of this kind?

The Personal Video Study Group

A video study group can respond to personal choices. It leads participants to engage in spontaneous narrative, including narrative about their own experience (Cizek 1995; Clandinin and Connelly 1996; Tochon 1994). In cases like these, the study group discussion workshop becomes the equivalent of a growth workshop.

The variety of viewpoints on the subjects discussed should be recognized as a source of enrichment, but the group must first come to an agreement on an ethic: an art of behavior in company. (Ethics and ideology are separated by a very thin veil, which reveals a paradox: that ethics includes the art of refraining from imposition. But are ethics committees subject to an ideology?) One way of avoiding potential abuse of such education for growth is to entrust facilitation of the study group to the participants in a regular round-robin and to confront any ideological imperialism that comes to the fore.

A video study group confronts the individual with her or his self-image. The video mirror can be adapted to serve several forms of self-evaluation. Participants explore their personal development. Emphasis is placed on the quality of personal reflection and on the individualization of interactions. One's personal way of setting the stage for knowledge is particularly important to this approach. The truth is, personal dynamics within the professional context represent the missing piece of the puzzle in initial education, as pointed out by Baxter (1991). This gap leads participants to develop situation-free cognitions. In contrast, the video study group is centered on lived, identity-producing experience; its approach is qualitative (Eisner 1988). Shared narratives allow for models of enhanced professionalism that prove useful in providing a neat image of the educational world (Barone 1992). Video representations of action provide new understanding of professional situations: image is insight (Perkins 1995).

Over the course of study group meetings, a shared life-narrative is progressively formed, like a story that participants jointly weave out of their discussions and their experiences in order to better understand and better know themselves. Thus, the approach of the individual narrative is in stark contrast to technical, rational educational models. The experiential perspective adopted implies that the subject of consciousness cannot be distinguished from the consciousness that gives birth to it, which means that knowledge itself cannot be fixed as an object. Growth is based on commitment, and sharing consists of work on subjectivity. It can take the following directions:

- Create a climate of confidence; elicit curiosity; supply documentation that relates to people's interests.

- Build the discussion around personal perspectives and problems; bring out motivations, needs, values; orient the discussion around questions of identity (who was I, who am I, who do I want to become?).

- Explore the relationship between cognition and affectivity; share feelings about action; bring attitudes to awareness; specify your self-image; discover yourself and get to know and share yourself.

- Explore situations involving aggression; analyze your own defense mechanisms; evaluate satisfaction; develop the affective.

- Make use of interpersonal resources and creativity; develop personal and social skills.

Example 5: Integrating the personal frame

Paul is responsible for the training of amateur ice hockey coaches. These coaches are responsible for teams of children and teenagers outside of school. Because Paul is dissatisfied with the usual methods of teaching intervention in hockey (presentation of the subject, instructions for execution, observation of players' performance, reaction to performance), he has organized a video study group with a personal frame. Each member recounts his experiences, illustrates them using the coaching session, and ties them in with his own feelings and his own life experiences. For the first meeting, every member brings a video clip of his choice that will illustrate his feelings about coaching.

Within the video study group, a stronger link begins to form between the professional and the personal domains. The coaches describe their own practice while visualizing it with their eyes closed. For the second meeting, groups are formed, with peer facilitators. The groups suggest strategies for the next game and present them on screen. The coaches draw up their intervention plans together. They make a diagram of the skating rink, locate the goals, the circles, and the lines on the ice, and they place the team members: the puck carrier, the defense. They show how they're going to group their players, where they'll be positioned, but also how their personalities and experiences might lead them to react.

Then the coaches tell each other about their own experiences. The reasons for their decisions seem to be socioaffective and to depend on the situation. They admit to Paul that in a league game, they have to win or parents become demotivated and stop sending their children for coaching. Yet in a coaching situation, every player must be given a chance and allowed the opportunity to pile up small victories. Nevertheless, when watching tapes of coaching sessions, Paul observes that the coaches don't interact with all the children, and that their instructions are far from clear.

Paul decides to help them improve this situation by having them put themselves in the youngsters' place. They start to tell how they began playing ice hockey, and they recall their early difficulties. They bring videotapes of game-preparation sessions and comment on them. They reach the point where they question the practices for early hockey training that left a stamp on them. By adopting a personal and more attentive teaching approach with the youngsters, they will achieve better team solidarity.

Teams are in training. The coaches start to introduce this more personal approach. For the first time, the young players are brought together for a roundtable discussion. The last game is screened. "How did you feel during the last game?" "Was everybody's attitude OK?" "What are your relationships with each other?" "Why?" The young people recount their emotions and talk about what frustrated them. They share their way of seeing and their way of living. They say that they chose hockey as a sport so they could talk in the locker room before and after practice. Thus, the coaches' goal of imposing quiet in the locker room appears counterproductive (Trudel, Haughian, and Gilbert 1996). They will keep that in mind.

The videotapes are placed in a cupboard so that they can be used for examples of successful tactics. Anyone can have access to them. The young people organize evenings when they screen the videotapes and form small groups to talk to each other about their exploits. This time for sharing further stimulates their intrinsic motivation. And so not just the coaches but the young players are engaged in research.

The coaches meet again and reflect on the implications of these personal experiences. They tie them to their own life-projects. Registration is on the increase — and the video study group has just enrolled its first women's hockey coach.

Personal operation

In the case described above, the coaches decided among themselves to integrate the personal approach into the teams they coach and into their work. They could have chosen other frames.

It's possible to have a personally based workshop in a video study group without members' own actions being subject to the same frame of reflection. It's possible to organize a personal workshop on strategic or sociocritical actions, for example. The frame for discussion provides *a point of view on one's point of view* on practice and wards off the impossibility of a final standpoint on meaning. The action frame is situated by the education frame.

Have you developed methods in your interventions for linking the subject matter to interactors' experience? Why is it important to recognize interactors' frustrations early? How can you benefit from this voicing of the personal to improve your interactions and as an intervenor? How can the narrative of lived experience be integrated without leading to interference in individuals' private lives?

Personal practice

▼ Review your disciplinary or professional curriculum and highlight the competencies that could be developed by means of a personal learning orientation. Make a list of possible opportunities. List them in order of importance. Try out the first ones.

▼ When your students are on a school outing with an educational goal, or when your students are about to begin a practicum or internship, ask them to tell you about their experiences, their doubts, and their questions. Suggest that they speak to professionals in the field. They should be required to bring to the fore cases experienced by people working in the field.

▼ Some cases provide an especially good illustration of the process you want to start. Using them as a basis, you could build an inventory of suitable cases for scene-setting at the start of a lesson. Group the cases by theme. Link them to the subject matter being broached. Present them to your learning groups as problems to be solved. This will teach your learners to reflect on experience.

▼ Derive from this a project that ties in with the interests of the students in the groups. These projects will allow for the resolution of larger problems. They should come together in a final, well-organized experience. In this way, you'll integrate everything — cases and problem-based learning — into a more all-encompassing narrative approach centered on personal experience.

The Pragmatic Video Study Group

There is a current resurgence of pragmatism among social theorists and educators. It offers a response to postmodernism. Some of its key features are (Hytten 1997):

- A call for a clear and balanced relationship between theory and practice.

- A call for the social responsibility of intellectuals and for the relevance of philosophy to day-to-day life.

- A call to make a tangible impact on the present and build the future.

- A sense of education for a democratic society.

- A call for the interpenetration of individual and so-cietal needs by means of networked participatory communities of researchers and developers.

Discussion conducted within a pragmatic frame is centered on the "why" that subtends the "how," rather than on the "what." The question asked is: "Why does one act in such-and-such a fashion?" Work on intentionality is fundamental to the pragmatic frame. It leads to the specification of intentions within their context and to reflection on the implications of acts. Professional discussion about intentions and actions elucidates the motives for action. Such discussion flows from a process rather than a method, a process whose key moments are:

- Self-observation (seeing oneself act)

- Achieving awareness (perceiving oneself)

- Diagnostic identification (analytic self-evaluation)

- Adjustment (corrective transformation).

In a pragmatic frame, interaction professions are analyzed as complex sets of intentional acts that relate to the communication of knowledge, know-how, and self-knowledge. The professional act is a function of a sender and one or several receivers. It relates to a message conveyed within a specific communicative context using a verbal code (the language), nonverbal codes (physical, inflectional, and gestural), and audiovisual or analog channels (graphic symbols, sounds, images).

Video education "revisited" (Collay 1991) through pragmatism should be able to adjust to differentiated and better situated learning needs, and that is just the advantage offered by the pragmatic video study group. Every member brings her or his own tapes, and together members confront, compare, discuss, reflect, and decide on change. The point is not just to internalize physical actions, but to compare several possible actions in order to build a practical and flexible model that can then be adapted to various situations. In a pragmatic frame, theory becomes practical and multiple; it is based in reflection using unique cases (Schön 1991). Thus, it is more descriptive, although its functional orientation is inspired by technical and essentially prescriptive rationality.

Pragmatic video pedagogy thus constitutes a language act and a constitutive practice of action research. It works on the semantics of action and behaviors (Garrison 1994). The video study group allows for the elucidation of knowledge about action. What is involved is a process of progressive explicitation. Thus, practical arguments are explored and elicited (Fenstermacher and Richardson 1993). Shared reflection on tacit knowledge emerging from practice leads to modeling of that knowledge.

Thanks to feedback, the pragmatic study group operates on the principle of emergence. Initiatives and new knowledge emerge from the recorded action in search of meaning. The process of research is implied rather than applied. Education emerges from conversations on action, rather than from previously fixed principles modeled on the basis of research results. Most often, verbalization of professional thinking underpins analysis and allows reflection to advance. Research in this context is different. The whole underlying logic of the recorded approach changes from a technocentric paradigm to a paradigm of reflective intention. Research rests on communication (and communication about communication) to make continuous change, owing to a process of definition of the arguments that account for and explain practice.

Pragmatic video pedagogy is thus centered on the meaning relationship and its intentionality within a project. The professional relationship implies a high degree of complexity management. The video study group allows one to handle the complexity of real-life situations. It's not really possible to isolate the variables in this complexity, to assess the long-term impact of this kind of professionalization. What's at issue here is the acquisition of life skills. From the moment one focuses on developing pragmatic elements and grasps complex settings freighted with implicit meaning, the measurement of performance can no longer suffice. A video study group conceived through action research models itself continuously on emerging needs.

Example 6: Integrating the pragmatic frame

Elizabeth is a resource teacher. The Department of Education has assigned her to supervise curricular change in a group of eight regional schools. To bring this about, she decides to rely on a pragmatic orientation. Elizabeth meets with the elementary school teachers in a roundtable session one Wednesday afternoon per month. At the end of the roundtable, the teachers present a summary of their notes before the camera, giving a general sense of their impressions and offering their opinions in the course of a brief video report. The videotape of all the teachers lasts twenty minutes or so. A copy is made of it, and the two copies circulate in schools and come back to the source school.

At first, the inquiry focuses on perceptions of the reading programs. At the start of the investigation, there is a strong tendency in favor of traditional positions. Elizabeth goes into the matter more deeply with the teachers: What do they do in their classrooms, when, why, and how? During this phase of elucidation of action, it appears that their practices are innovative but that the teachers don't dare invoke a theoretical frame of reference, because to some extent it eludes them and mastery of it appears to be a matter for specialists. The liberty granted to students in the activity method seems to them to be interesting, but they require a guarantee before they will take the plunge.

What would you do in their place to initiate change?

Every meeting begins with a screening of videotapes from at least two schools (forty minutes); everyone takes notes. Subsequent discussion explores more deeply the observations made by the teachers from the other schools. Next comes the theme of the day. In some schools, a theme program has been set up. In others, the theme of the next meeting is chosen at the end of the current meeting, just before videotaping begins. The themes addressed resonate from one school to another. Ties are forged.

These teachers have decided to form a team. Over the course of the meetings, they have found that they have assimilated better than they realized the frame put before them as part of the reform that's under way. They now feel more confident about braving a change in certain aspects of their teaching, and even about modifying the proposed reforms. They adapt them to their own teaching contexts. They realize that academic change does not rely on acceptance of doctrine, but on a set of flexible, evolving, reflective practices.

In these schools, a group has come together. The teachers textualize their practice. These texts become reference points for other schools and other groups of teachers, before whom they are called to contextualize the information. Thus, this group of teachers progressively defines a new sphere of action. When, after two years, they report their perceptions to Elizabeth, their theoretical position has changed. They are more assured, and they have the courage to test the knowledge transmitted by the Department of Education. They do test it, and they improve what is proposed to them. They construct knowledge through practice. These teachers are tapped into for research; they are consulted on the process they have been through.

Pragmatic operation

What Elizabeth does with other teachers, you can do among your peers. Why not implement a similar approach with two of your coworkers?

- Take one aspect of your field and, together, plan new reflective experiences that will abound in experiential learning. Build an interactive process, one that is flexible and that suits the participants' level, and into which video feedback would integrate successfully.

- Discuss the process with your peers, prepare it, and ask them for their advice. Link the planned process to the ideal self of the participants involved. Make the connection between the participants' projects and videotape; point out that it could be useful to them in the realization of their own goals. Create one or several video study group sessions within special interest groups.

- Implement what you have planned. Set up feedback modes among the participants and with your two coworkers. Provide each other with follow-up.

- If possible, sit in on some of your coworkers' activities and have them come into your own setting.

Discuss what you see. Improve your interventions by taking account of their comments.

- Share your evaluations. Blend two settings for a given activity. For another activity, use the space differently. Create theme-based interest groups by means of a registration system.

Organize a mini-conference for the participants, with workshops and video presentations.

Pragmatic practice

▼ Make use of videotape in student assignments. Call upon your students to present arguments orally, to organize themselves, and to plan activities on tape. Call on them to present taped reports of readings, and syntheses. And why limit yourself to written texts? Students could also express the thoughts they have when preparing an activity, at a key point in their work, or during a problem-solving phase.

▼ Take advantage of students' initiatives and wishes. Invite them to manage one part of the organization in order to better meet their own needs.

▼ If you have too many students in your class to conduct a reflective process, find a constructive way to reduce the number. Ask for two rooms; work on a rotational system; assign independent study to one-third of the class. Reflection is hard where receptiveness is lacking. Before teaching reflection, one must set up the conditions necessary for one's own intellectual and affective receptiveness. If you set up two groups, alternate their screenings.

▼ In order not to lose the ideas that come to you at moments of inspiration, record them on Dictaphone. At any time of day, plan by thinking out loud. You can do it in the car, in the garden, and during quiet moments in the morning or evening. Listen to a melody you love and give yourself up to inspiration. Ask yourself: What can I do to help my students reflect better and more adequately?

▼ How can you go about eliciting reflection from them? Call to mind the times when this worked well. Why did it work well? How?

How could you recreate the conditions? Can it be integrated into video feedback? Try to elucidate your own practice; lead your students to verbalize theirs on video.

Verbalizing one's practice requires reflection. Reflection requires practice.

Some Important Points

To speak of video pedagogy is to speak of various types of feedback, carried out through interactive practice, in line with a frame for discussion. This book does not include, in the definition of video pedagogy, the equally important practices for preparing audiovisual materials specific to particular disciplines (for example, documentaries in biology). These merit discussion on their own. As well, the multiplicity of valid frames for discussion for video pedagogy does not mean that it is OK to do anything, anyhow, in this field. The presence of the camera is not sufficient to trigger awareness raising. Further, although the frames for discussion presented often contain points of compatibility and are indeed, to some extent, complementary, it is not recommended that approaches be blended.

The fact is that, to achieve coherent education or change, most often the best approach is to gain in-depth knowledge of a single perspective and to internalize it without being dogmatic. Each perspective has its value and reveals a given aspect of professional practice on which one can work with a view to reflective development. Every frame for discussion corresponds to a certain descriptive vocabulary and a way of envisaging reflective action that is solidly founded and cohesive. The frame for discussion and the vocabulary that goes with it are, first and foremost, tools for conceptualizing practice. What matters is practical professional development, whatever the theoretical tools one uses — but theoretical tools are indispensable.

Video assistance plays a mediating role between theoretical professional development and the profession's real-life setting. In initial professional education, nothing can replace true practice and its concomitant full professional responsibility. The video study group comes into play as a mediating force, providing the necessary adjustments within professional development. Discussion of the videotaped image constitutes a useful regulator — indeed, one that is indispensable to those wishing to develop relational skills. It is a powerful tool for focusing attention on key elements of the profession, providing it is clear that these elements must not be severed from others. With the video study group it is possible to focus attention better on certain relational events and on needed additional information emerging from professional education, but without neglecting other events. The whole is done in such a way that discussion about experience can come within the framework of professional situations.

In this way, the shock of working in the field is attenuated. Participants benefit from the support of their partners. For professionals who already enjoy a degree of experience, discussion of videotaped professional interactions allows for the achievement of a better fit between one's theory and one's practice and can create a climate favorable to reflective, shared change. In professional development, video feedback is probably the best tool currently available for reflection and adjustment.

In Brief

In this chapter, we have seen that in a video study group, discussion can be broached from several perspectives:

- *Functional discussion* relates to the effectiveness of action and mastery of action. It is centered on the results of the task to be accomplished. Sessions unfold in line with objectives that have been specified in performance terms.

- *Strategic discussion* emphasizes method of work, methodological learning, and the conceptual structures of learning. Implementation of plans, interactive decisions, cognitive styles, and the mental strategies

used to solve problems are among the most promi-
nent topics.

- *Constructivist discussion* elicits awareness raising based
  on authentic experiences. Its foundations consist of
  shared learning, and it challenges prior conceptions,
  provokes cognitive conflict, and models situations
  by analogy.

- *Sociocritical discussion* denounces the abuse of power
  inherent in language and social stereotypes as per-
  petuated through education. Using a social, democratic, and participatory perspective, it empowers
  the learner in order to promote her or his emancipation (adopting a feminist, ethical, ecological, ethnic,
  or social critique).

- *Personal or narrative discussion* underpins the autobiographical and narrative approaches to human experience. It is centered on personal growth, and it
  operates in line with a humanist, phenomenological,
  psychoanalytic, or spiritual approach.

- *Pragmatic discussion* is centered on the explicitation
  of the motives for action. Practical arguments tied
  to intentions allow for a grasp of the impact of
  situations on knowledge. In this perspective, help-
  ing the other to know links know-how to knowledge.

It is the frame for discussion that determines the meaning of the
vocabulary used. Can this really be objectified? There is a paradigm
inherent in talking of a frame for discussion as though it could be
located on the outside. The final, eclectic chapter of this book deals
with supporting participants' experiences within the video study
group.

CHAPTER FOUR

Supporting Interaction

When a reflective perspective is adopted for education, professional development, and change, participants alternate acting and reflecting. The double progress from knowledge to action and from know-how to verbal expression ties theory to practice. In this way, practical knowledge is developed and one's colleagues in the video study group become a part of the reflection.

What, then, is the role of the supervisor or mentor? This role has changed. In this chapter, some principles are presented on which counseling of video study group participants can be based. The operative notions are those of support and counsel, rather than of supervision. Support adapts to participants' needs. Since activity regulation is shared, it is integrated into facilitation and counseling.

A Regulatory Vision of Support

In this section, we'll be dealing with the context for the regulation of a video study group. The word "regulation" should be understood here to mean "adjustment," the way a thermostat regulates room temperature through feedback. Support consists of supervision between peers and includes no sense of hierarchy. The fact that the support occurs in a fairly defined context, that of video feedback, does not mean that you are freed up from considerations relating to supervision in general. Learners help each other plan their professional interactions, undertake educational activities, manage them, and reflect on future improvements.

The mentor invites each group to name a peer facilitator. During this stage of help with planning, the mentor supplies peer facilitators with documentation and a set of potentially useful strategies and tools and suggests critical indices that enable one to decide when to use them. As the peer facilitator engages the group in activity, the mentor helps her or him to diagnose problems that may arise by relating the group's intentions to the methods of organization chosen. Observation of recorded sequences made by fellow learners complements this aid, along with professional experiences conducted collaboratively (in pairs within a single work unit) and indications supplied by the reactions of those receiving the intervention and of other learners when they screen the video clips. Facilitation interviews are also to be videotaped, thus providing the basis for reflection activities on the peer regulation of the video study group. Several levels of feedback are layered upon one another and interact with one another, and the videotapes constitute a memory of experience and change.

Managing an educational relationship is a complex activity, and it takes time to learn the variables that will facilitate the management of unexpected situations. Within this process, the quality of observation conducted plays a major role. Quality will be enhanced through systematic objectification. Objectification should relate to planning, action, modeling of action, and modeling of one's own reflection.

Objectifying reflection is alternately a retrospective and prospective process. It prompts repeated comings and goings in time, and it compares events using categories of significance progressively built by the learner. At this stage, the person in charge of the video study group acts as the peer facilitators' consultant. She or he is called upon as needed. The role of the peer facilitators is to help with the modeling and analysis of action within the group — not in preset terms, but in response to participants' remarks, and by employing terms used spontaneously to allow everyone to specify her or his reflection on the videotaped actions. For the mentor, it is a delicate matter not to act as an outside authority during this modeling phase, because participants must have their own sense of what is appropriate and thus develop an internal authority that springs from experience.

Shared observation

Interaction covers numerous kinds of learning. Participants need to learn which among the many processes inherent in human relations will allow for the fulfillment of certain kinds of intention; integrate and combine these processes into coherent strategies; decode situations and manage them as they arise; increase their awareness of the implications of the present moment for the future; and anticipate, act, and respond without losing sight of their goals.

At the start, all of this is very vague. The novice learner begins with an ideal of the profession and a set of values and fears that must be disentangled.

With this in mind, groups organize their resources. They bring together a set of experience-based data; certain recorded data will serve as reference points for modeling practical professional thinking. Groups choose an approach to observation that suits their goals and the targeted discipline and level. They practice systematic observation in order to forge links among participants' experiences. Each participant has a role.

Among methods of observation currently used, here are some that might be mentioned to peer facilitators (Acheson and Gall 1992):

- A list of interactional behaviors is a useful indicator. For example, verbal exchanges can be studied in terms of the angles in the workplace, mastery of space and time, location of interaction (where the interactors are situated), and who the privileged interactors are (their sex, age, provenance, culture, and social class).

- Word-for-word transcription of certain video clips can help participants become aware of their oral delivery.

Choose the elements that could benefit from change, and bear in mind that not everything can be changed. Word-for-word transcription allows for elucidation of the components of certain dialogue situations, while examining the impact of questions and answers. On the other hand, this method of observation cannot take into account the historic and spatial context of the dialogue.

- A listing of participants' questions provides abundant information on dialogue management and on the personalization of professional relations:

  Are the questions prepared for, foreshadowed?

  To which cognitive level is the participant's discourse addressed (memory, comprehension, application, analysis, synthesis, or evaluation)? (Note: Video analysis tools for discourse analysis open up fascinating perspectives [Roschelle 1995; Goldman Segall 1991, 467-497].)

- What is the quality of the information supplied to the interactor?

  Are poorly understood questions reworded?

  Is the professional using an exploratory approach and the stages of the deepening process?

  Are questions and items of information often repeated, whether in the same form or in content? If so, interactors may no longer respond to such formulaic questions.

- A listing of participants' answers is equally important:

  What is the quality of feedback provided to interactors within the professional situation?

  In what socioaffective climate does the feedback operate? For example, does the response to an incorrect answer include negative reinforcement?

The more directive the interaction, the less the feedback. Does the participant ask interlocutors for their opinion and help them with their arguments?

Does the participant provide a point of view on the explanations and arguments produced? What is that point of view?

Feedback can serve to modify the concept produced by reformulating it, by applying the concept while extending analysis, by comparing the concepts expressed, or by summarizing the concepts put forth by the interlocutors.

Are the responses detailed or cryptic?

Do the responses validate the interlocutors? Validation must be occasional, specific, spontaneous, and credible; and to be effective, it must respect specific criteria. It informs the interlocutor of her or his competence, orients her or him in light of earlier success, and, by emphasizing effort, fosters future projects and successes.

- A listing of structural data about the organization of interaction will indicate whether the participant and the interlocutors are aware of the key points in the articulation of the contents presented:

Does the professional operating in a professional interaction situation summarize subject matter dealt with earlier when establishing links with new content? or example, does the negotiator help a potential client to make a bridge between earlier negotiations and the present situation?

Does the interlocutor have an overview of subject matter or decisions upcoming?

Has time been taken to situate the interlocutor's role?

What transition markers does the professional use?

Does the professional emphasize essential points with special gestures or behaviors?

Is a visual overview available? Interaction and the articulation of discourse are associated with structural elements, and often rules for behavior can be set out that anticipate possible problems.

- A listing of the number of interactors who really engage with the goal of the interaction, as well as a listing of interlocutors' movements, also provides interesting information that can serve as the basis for reflection and professional decision making.

The goals of shared facilitation

The role of the peer facilitator extends to all aspects of the video study group's operation. The peer facilitator provides feedback on videotapes, but also on the preparation of the interactions that are taped and on the experience narrative recounted following the video study group's meetings. To foster positive interdependence within the group, the peer facilitator assigns responsibilities to individual participants. For example, the task of one is to motivate participants to express themselves; another is called upon to recap major ideas; a third presents the group report (Abrami et al. 1993).

The various means for reflective professionalization can truly work only if peer facilitators and their partners are actively interested in others' experiences and intervene with regard to the experiences of whichever participant has the floor. The whole group must get involved in feedback. Whether it be during the individual interview or during the group workshop, peer facilitators must bear in mind their major goals in relation to the other participants: to support and facilitate, to raise awareness, and to conceptualize experience with a view to future action (Tomlinson 1995). The mentor helps peer facilitators who are experiencing difficulty and monitors the rotation of roles and functions. As they develop as peer facilitators, participants learn a new aspect of professional interaction.

Participants arrive at the video study group with individual priorities of their own. The more closely meetings answer to their own values and their inner motives, the greater their involvement will be. For this reason, at the outset, facilitation consists of elucidating participants' inner motives. The fact is, it's only possible to understand participants' feelings to the extent that the context for those feelings and their underlying models of reality have been subject to discussion. Each participant reacts on the basis of presuppositions. It's good to put these on the table right from the start.

From that point on, the group will develop meaningful activities — activities that the peer facilitator or mentor would themselves enjoy being involved in, that would concern them personally. It is not recommended that one plunge into activities one does not believe in. Minimal intellectual and moral allegiance is necessary to render the meetings dynamic. Once one has noticed that an activity is becoming artificial, it is better to find a more significant one, or to find a means of reinjecting life into something that has become too routine.

Consistency between personal and professional activity is important. From this consistency derives participants' ability to motivate themselves. Peer facilitators themselves are situated in a relationship of support and counseling. In order to motivate participants, raise their awareness, and help them conceptualize their experience, peer facilitators must develop at least three aspects of support: they must reduce stress related to the profession and to change, engage in active listening with participants, and share experiences. These aspects are described below.

Stress, truth, and videotape

To provide support means to reduce participants' anxieties and any tensions that may arise among them. Sometimes participants begin the educational process with considerable fear; and they cling to their self-esteem above all. Right from the very first video recordings, they risk losing face. They become aware of their bodies, their gestural habits; they come to hate their voices; and they envy the natural ability or the natural ease of the rare photogenic members of the group. The presence of the mentor or the peer facilitator has the potential to wound or to comfort.

Put yourself in their place. Consider that, especially in initial education, they are being confronted, probably for the first time, with their professional potential. Are they worth anything on the labor market? Will they find a job? Will they be able to withstand the rhythm of preparation and institutional demands, not to mention sometimes difficult interactions with — depending on their profession — students, coworkers, and professional role models? Don't add further tension; at this stage, a wounding remark could actually slow down the progress of a career. Ensure that peer facilitators exercise the same tact.

Whether it be in a context of education, professional development, or change, every participant wishes to appear competent and solid and wishes to control the situation. Newness, insecurity, and doubt are contributors to stress — the stress we are all inclined to deny if the subject is broached too candidly: "Who, me? Are you kidding?" The intensity of the stress will depend on the complexity of the situation with which we are faced. In contradictory situations, we are torn, and it feels as though we are struggling against a part of ourselves. Sometimes the appearance of mastery makes it easier to acquire real competence in a professional situation. And, of course, we are all entitled to our own criteria for success. If success were completely subject to the guidance of others, it would risk becoming others' success. Indeed, true success may consist of freeing oneself up from other people's criteria.

Systems for supervising novice workers in educational institutions complicate the situation still further. These systems are often based on external criteria that have little to do with the inner satisfaction indicating success. New practitioners are controlled by means that veterans would have little liking for if they had to face them. Right from the start, novice professionals are placed in a stressful situation, without having the time to grasp that they are being evaluated, weighed, and judged — without even having realized that they are in the hot seat. What is owed by the person who provides support is to reduce the pressure by making it relative.

This is where the comparatively unthreatening idea of support and counsel comes in.

The person in charge of a video study group is conscious of wearing two hats: that of the educator and that of the evaluator. In one sense, she or he is as deeply chagrined by this as the learner and tries to do what is best. Having experienced this stress, she or he understands it, knowing that it makes people negative, anxious, and distrustful, and that it sometimes leads them to regress to the only tactics they trust, even while knowing these tactics are unacceptable and have been outgrown.

Stress makes us rash and irrational and leads to distortion in our perception of events. In such circumstances, people will seek refuge in conversational arguments that simply betray how hard it is to face up: "This wouldn't have happened in my other group." "But what happened to Mary was even worse ..." Learners' reality buckles: "The photocopier wasn't working." "The principal was just there by chance." "I didn't really insult him." They do their best to return things to normal: "Oh, of course, I noticed that." "Oh, what's the good of bringing that up again?" "So on top of everything, you have to explain every little thing to them?" Finally, learners find excuses: "It didn't work out, but the interaction was good." "He was very impolite. I had to shout so that he would understand." "They were so importunate, I preferred to keep my distance. They know how to get along by themselves." (A close examination of related situations is presented by Tomlinson [1995].)

Mentors know that these characteristics due to stress can be detected in their own behavior. It's better to face up to this than to defend oneself against it. Avoidance strategies take root all too soon. Just as the learner is new to the video study group, mentors are confronted with new groups and unforeseen surprises, with adults who are touchier than children, with criticisms that challenge their competence, with perceptive minds that pinpoint their weak spots, and with mischief-making coworkers who love spreading rumors and whose penchant for fiction knows no bounds. Despite all these hazards, the educational mentors learn how to preserve their motivation and faith and, sometimes, how to transmit them. Those who continue taking an interest in their work probably do so because they consider it more of an art than an occupation.

An understanding of learners' stress helps them to recognize their own tendency to regress toward easier strategies, and this awareness facilitates the performance of the second function of support: listening that provides the basis for raising awareness.

Listening to raise awareness

Human action betrays that awareness is limited by sometimes very personal perspectives. Because its field is defined, consciousness is selective. We only grasp reality on the basis of prior concepts and mental constructs. Previous knowledge and experience are terribly influential in the analysis of new situations. At a very young age, we learn to select what and how we will perceive.

In general, with very few exceptions, we human beings tend to be very interested in ourselves and not very interested in others unless they can be of use to us. This is a problem one must face right from the start of the video study group's meetings. If you grant that every learner adores talking about "number one," then it's clear that listening to others may become boring, not to mention painful.

The mentor and peer facilitators must expect to hear a good deal from others and to speak very little about themselves. Since listening is a selective activity, if there is no a real will to listen to what is said, not much will be gained by it. Without true attention to what is going on, meetings will progress toward a gentle lethargy, due to the fragmentary perception of a few amusing episodes welded together with personal musings. As well, the reflection workshop and the logbook will become the place where participants learn to lie: to say exactly what it takes for the mentor, the peer facilitator, or other participants to be satisfied with appearances. And last, in their turn, the semantic networks and cognitive maps produced in the process of education will become the instruments for phony perception. Their falsely structured organization will hide the chaos of professional events.

Awareness raising proceeds, then, through listening (and not phony listening), the look (a look that seeks to see and understand), and sensitivity to context. Motivation, attention, and awareness render activities educational and justify having brought people together for education research. When motivation and attention are present, it is possible to begin conceptualizing experience with a view to future action.

Analogies and conceptualization

Support means sharing experiences and making meaning from them. In order to do so, one must conceptualize the experience and give words to tacit, daily behavior. Analogy can help. Within a video study group, the reflective group operates along the same lines as in professional situations. Conceptualization of the professional act develops through a definition of situations and their reflection within the group. The latter is facilitated if instructions are clear. Little by little, one's explanatory gray areas are defined. One begins by defining one's terms and the events that arise during screenings. One establishes parallels between the situations experienced by participants and the circumstances of education, professional development, or change within the reflective group.

Naming events, in itself, lays out possible methods of resolution. Often, analogies aid in the conceptualization of professional situations. For example, a participant, a teacher, or an educational mentor who lets slip an opportunity to explain her or his position will see the impact of the problem or plea increase the next time it comes around.

Similarly, peer facilitators must acknowledge unspoken messages and express their positions as soon as an event requires it — that is, if they do not wish to deal with overwhelming problems. Like that of any professional interactor, the peer facilitator's position might be to postpone making a decision or to allow participants to make the appropriate choice. But if so, it must be made clear that this apparent *laissez-faire* approach is in fact thought out, willed, and conscious. Around a table in the shared-reflection workshop, numerous nonverbal appeals can be detected at the same time. In order to avoid cognitive overload, both the mentor and the peer facilitator must have their strategies for response. By assuming leadership turn and turn about, participants learn to negotiate interaction, and they assert themselves.

Let's look a little closer at this parallel between professional interaction and the interactions experienced within the video study group. Strategies that can be envisaged in the video study group are the same as those useful in professional interaction: deferred response ("I can't answer you just now; we'll come back to that in a moment"); response with an anecdote (a story that has nothing to do with the case yet is obliquely significant); problem solving; strategic use of obstacles; and so on. Little by little, a better definition of professional situations, and the imponderables that go into them, leads to the specification of possible strategies and actions.

Ethical issues must be addressed head-on — for instance, the issue of criteria for differentiating interaction from manipulation. The mentor and peer facilitator must ensure that the principles put forward do not clash with their own interaction strategies. Learners will expect consistency between theory and action as a minimum (and it's a minimum that makes a good part of current educational practice look somewhat lacking!).

Conceptualization activities are grafted onto feedback in the process of education. Formative feedback, in which the basic aspects of support are manifested (motivating, reducing stress, listening to raise awareness, and sharing with a view to future experience) come into play according to one of two modes within the video study group: as individual interviews and in the group shared-reflection workshop.

Let's first take a look at the individual reflective interview.

The individual reflective interview

The video study group offers several types of activity in rotation. The individual interview is one of them. The interview may be conducted by the mentor, or it can be delegated to the peer facilitator. It's also possible to organize individual interviews in rotation and cooperatively among learners, with each one being responsible for a particular theme ("expert" method). All three of these formulas may be used together.

The retroactive individual interview often follows observation within a professional situation, but it can also be practiced in alternation with group workshop interviews. The individual interview must satisfy a certain logic and continuity determined by consensus. It can be governed by themes broached in succession (preparation for professional interaction, questions, answers, management of interaction, and so on).

The interview unfolds in predetermined stages. For example, it gets started by dealing with questions related to receptivity, to the previous interview, and to the degree of motivation for pursuing reflection. It proceeds by specifying a subject on which attention will be focused during the session. This subject is fully clarified so that all are assured of a clear understanding of the object of reflection (Villeneuve 1994).

The session can be conceived as a project for analysis aimed at fulfilling specific needs of one or more learners: how does the proposed interaction project for this session harmonize with the group project and participants' ideal selves? The mentor, peer facilitator, or helping-learner must then be careful not to bruise the interlocutor's sensitivities; in bringing this person to reflect upon the appropriateness of classifying professional actions in order to better understand them, they are experimenting with a live subject. At issue are the videotaped actions of a human, sensitive person, which all are examining together. This necessarily has an impact on the individual's sense of identity and self-esteem.

The data recorded lead to a specification of choices and orientations by formulating hypotheses with a view to future action. Reflection consists of revealing analytic plans implied in and by professional acts. The purpose of identifying the connections between acts made on these different levels is to increase the learner's perceptual acuteness. In this way, learners will, little by little, become more capable of observation, and their observation will become to some extent operational. They will more easily identify the right indices, in the right place, at the right time, and they will better relate these indices to strategies and anticipate their results.

At the end of the interview, the group can set goals (who, what, when, how?) and evaluate the session.

The group reflective interview

A second mode of support and feedback within the video study group is the group interview. Some of the components that are valid in the individual interview can also form a part of the group reflective interview. Reflection in a small group, following selective screening of a video clip, can adopt a process of deepening understanding in successive levels. Here is just one example (Note: The process presented here is different from the DIDEOR model presented in Chapter Two. It is based on a proposal by Paré and Auclair [1988]):

A. A participant focuses her attention on the subject while releasing tension. She listens to and watches the tape in a state of alertness and relaxation. Then she chooses a passage upon which she wishes to comment, in order to describe it briefly in writing.

B. The participant reconstructs the chosen clip and reconstitutes its context in an informative and descriptive way.

C. Following this descriptive stretch, the participant expresses her feelings and her emotions in relation to what she has observed. She formulates a personal point of view. At this point, she visualizes her feelings in the form of a symbolic image or an analogy that illustrates her perception. Her inner and then shared dialogue with this symbol allow her to examine its implications.

D. Perceived in this fashion, the symbol becomes a means of specifying her perceptions of the professional act, and the action currently being analyzed, by initiating dialogue within the group. The image becomes a creative source of resources. On one hand, it produces communication of feelings and representations among participants; but further, it is creative of more essential actions, actions that are better guided by the participant's intuitive sense of what befits her.

E. Subsequently, the image takes on a day-to-day aspect, and the debate begins to focus on personal narratives of experience, avoiding any critique of the actions of the participant whose presentation has just been screened. The dialogue confronts various images of the action linked to the first person.

Whatever the process implemented for a shared analysis of the video recordings, the mentor must begin by defining the collaborative procedures each person will follow within the group. (Subsequently, collaborative action can be used to improve or modify these procedures.) Within the small-group reflection workshop, it's recommended that only brief, selected clips be screened. (Either participants or the mentor may choose them, in line with a predetermined theme or for a reason flowing from the events recorded.) Each clip may be viewed twice without commentary, so that participants can become familiar with it. This allows reflection to develop before group analysis begins (Tomlinson 1995). In offering commentary, the participant can identify at least two positive aspects of her or his recorded intervention. The whole activity is focused on supporting the learner making the presentation; other participants take care to avoid demoralizing that person.

This requirement must be very clear to the peer facilitators who bring the clips before their groups. It must be strongly emphasized that negative judgments are not appropriate at the moment when the group is seeking to jointly construct knowledge about action. If the participant who has been recorded has no positive comments to make, others can formulate some, or, as a last resort, the peer facilitator or mentor can do so. Subsequently, the individual learner may be asked if she or he sees particular points to which attention should be drawn. At that stage, various strategies for improving the situation as experienced by the learner can be analyzed.

Feedback and its observable components

We have looked at two modes of support within the video study group: the individual reflective interview and the group workshop that functions as an extension of the individual reflective interview. We have also seen that in each case, support aims to reduce participants' personal stress (as well as stress *among* participants), and that it promotes active listening and awareness raising by leading participants to conceptualize their experience.

Let's now deepen our understanding of the nature of feedback within the process of support. In an "open" interview, what are the topics of conversation?

In this section, I will indicate the importance of relating reflection to the observable components of each situation. Next, in the last two sections of the chapter, I will broach the role that semi-directive conversations can play in elucidating practice. Finally, I shall define experience as autonomous knowledge.

Like the individual interview, group feedback is based on data derived from observation. The participant must grasp that the feedback deals with stable, objective components of professional action. Remarks will carry all the more weight if they relate to concrete events and facts. The participant is brought to express and formulate her or his own point of view. It may happen that a participant will express anxieties. These often relate to a presumed lack or defect. Rather than treating these fears in an abstract, psychoanalytic fashion, it may be necessary to incorporate them into a fully concrete definition that makes solutions directly operational.

If the fear and those solutions that can be entertained are imprecise, then the anxiety may give rise to serious distress. In this situation, it is possible to respond to professional anxieties by working with participants to discover what behaviors they display that testify to there being nothing to worry about on this score. A participant's anxieties allow for the detection of genuine underlying problems and the pinning down of behaviors that are at their source; these often themselves lead to a solution. A participant who fears he lacks expressive warmth could be asked to describe the behavior of a professional who does display such expressive warmth. This descriptive process could be fine-tuned until it becomes operational — that is, the participant would faithfully present a possible action plan for expressing human warmth in his professional actions.

Thus, participants who express their fears can be asked to define the words they are using in order to see the situations with which these concepts are most closely associated. Participants will thereby be brought to translate their fears into concrete terms and lived experience.

A definition of behavior that is the reverse of the behavior feared will set criteria for the solution (Acheson and Gall 1992). Abstract terms that refer to positive professional behaviors can also be the subject of a concrete definition allowing participants to examine how, for instance, a seasoned professional manifests enthusiasm, or charisma, or goodwill, or consistency.

The important decisions in a participant's professional life can be discussed in the workshop, and thus be brought to a new level of awareness. The video study group can bring participants to make decisions that affect their personal lives: change their plans, undertakings, use of time, ways of doing things; eradicate certain behaviors, modify habits or attitudes; broaden their understanding of others and their knowledge. During the reflective interview, the peer facilitator or mentor should encourage the participant to envision an alternative whenever dissatisfaction is revealed. The peer facilitator or mentor will warn of the two main pitfalls: namely, the single hypothesis and the single solution, both equally reductionist (Acheson and Gall 1992). Observations are not subject to a single explanation, nor are problems subject to single solutions. Practice and the possibility for comparing experiences systematically facilitate the bringing to awareness of the real potential within professional action.

Once the conversation opens up to the whole group, a prerequisite must be set out: remarks are to be encouraging, and unkind comments should be avoided, even outside of meetings, in order to preserve the group's successful operation. At the end of a session, a summary of salient points is presented, and this can provide the basis for suggestions for the next session.

Another requirement that must be made of participants is that of preserving confidentiality. For instance, a mentor responsible for three groups (and remember that it's hard to operate with more than fifteen participants) must explicitly require that personal information shared within one group not be imparted to members of another group. (On the other hand, it is possible to have moments of synthesis about the principles that have been brought to light.) This provision, if duly respected, allows a participant who has been through a traumatic experience within a given group to join a new one, and thus be freed from the negative impression that partners in the first group may retain about her or his earlier experiences. In this way, the participant starts afresh.

The elucidation of practical knowledge

Considerable work has been done by the educational community to elucidate knowledge of action. Reflective action has become the *leitmotiv* of educational processes, professional development sessions, and current change. In this vein, numerous teacher-researchers have tried to formalize practical reflection (Schön 1991; Calgren, Handal, and Vaage 1994).

Research emerging from the fields of semiotics and the philosophy of education is also promising. For instance, some researchers (Fenstermacher and Richardson 1993) are studying the potential of argument analysis to help practitioners make reflective use of research and of professional experience. They are developing a strategy for education, professional development, and social change inspired by Aristotle. This strategy is centered on the explicitation of practical reasoning. The goal is to understand and explain action by elucidating the causal relations within professional thinking. Peer facilitators operating with this approach usually base their work on retrospective interviews.

Reflection is conducted on action that has already been done. Referring to Book VI, Chapter Seven, of Aristotle's *Nicomachean Ethics*, the peer facilitator helps the professional make the motives for her or his action explicit and rebuild her or his own practical syllogisms. In this context, the practical syllogism is defined as "a device that both illustrates the process of practical reasoning and formalizes that process" (Fenstermacher and Richardson 1993).

Reconstituting practical argumentation makes the workings of the activities of daily life explicit. In this process, the often somewhat dense thoughts of ordinary living serve as the basis for reconstituting practical arguments. Once the syllogisms have been articulated, they reveal professional rules for action. Little by little, the professional will lay out the premises of her or his action, revise them, and bring to light the foundations of her or his sensitivity-in-action. By articulating the logical propositions that guide action, she or he transforms know-how into self-knowledge.

Problem-solving researchers who work on the reconstitution of expert knowledge also refer to the elucidative (Socratic) conversation to inventory the rules and conditions for professionals' actions. My own work in this line of research has shown how the explicitation of the procedures for action allows for a comparison of these stages of pre-action and interaction, in order to study variability in professional action plans (Tochon and Dionne 1994). Cause-and-effect rules partly condition professional actions and reactions. However, the mobility of the rules for action does not always allow for identification of the triggers for the situations that arise.

In the field of human interaction, it may be an illusion to think that all knowledge about action can be made explicit. On one hand, it's not certain that knowledge about action can be translated into propositional knowledge without being denatured; and on the other hand, it may be that the situated know-how that is truly useful to professionals-in-training or in the process of professional development does not exist at the level of explicitation.

It is in just this context that the video study group can play an important role. Study group work is done on incorporated knowledge, knowledge of the image, participants' mental disposition, and their relations with each other. Work is done on several levels simultaneously toward socioaffective goals.

Experience as independent knowledge

Throughout this book, I have tried to show the tact with which professional knowledge must be elucidated, and how the individual's freedom to learn must be respected. By showing, in Chapter Three, that the frames for professional reflection are many in number, I drew attention to the fact that shared reflection only suggests interpretative models. Ultimately, it's up to individuals to build their own knowledge and interpret their professional situation in the most significant way. It's not always by using the words of others that one best illuminates one's own reality. Though we may have at our disposal useful tools and a whole kit of strategies suited to the situations that arise, we will feel at ease professionally only when we feel we can dip into a well of knowledge from our own experience and not that of others.

This subtle point leads certain researchers to propose that experiential knowledge constitutes *difference*. A difference cannot be expressed in terms of comparison and classification. A different knowledge, knowledge of another order, can hardly be expressed. Knowledge and the intrinsic differences among various kinds of knowledge can be analyzed in terms of authority (see the account provided by Munby and Russell 1994).

Traditionally, philosophy has distinguished the *authority of position* from the *authority of reason*. The *authority of position* suggests a certain mode of action on the basis of the fact that an authority has already stated the soundness of this action. In education, professional development, and change, the authority of position comes into play every time professionals are shown what to do and how to do it in such-and-such a situation. When young professionals engage in discussion with their seniors, they learn to conform to the authoritative positions their colleagues convey to them. Their colleagues' experience serves as a model for making decisions about how to act.

When colleagues or mentors act as authorities, it is on the basis of their personal experience. But their authority nevertheless forbids, to some extent, the beginner from assuming responsibility and developing her or his own authority. The very same problem arises in the professional development of experienced individuals and in planned change, whether in the business world or in an institutional setting.

In reflection workshops, another kind of authority develops: the *authority of reason*. By means of the elucidation of practice and the rationalization of knowledge about action, participants can formulate professional action in coherent, personal propositions. These propositions and professional rules are based on their authority of reason, an authority produced by their reflection *on* action. This constitutes a first step toward the appropriation of knowledge about action and professional emancipation. Once in their work setting, however, though these professionals may well subscribe to certain entrenched principles emerging from their reflection, they still find themselves *in action* — and to some extent, action as it unfolds is a handicap to reasoning.

The context of action proves to be more complex than is presumed by the coherent principles on which prior reflection relied. And professionals are called upon to free themselves up simultaneously from the yoke of the authority of position and the weight of the authority of reason. They must somehow manage to situate themselves in action and go beyond the models they have been shown, and they must do this in an unpremeditated fashion.

A major problem in initial education is the absence of external criteria for action. The devices of both position and reason are merely temporary props as one deals with the necessity to translate the responsibility for decision making into action. This "other" knowledge, this reflection *in* action, in itself constitutes a form of authority of a fundamentally different kind from that of the authorities of position and reason. It constitutes an authority that does not derive from others and that one cannot articulate in propositions: an *authority of experience* (Munby and Russell 1994).

The video study group institutes dialogue among these three types of authority in order to accelerate the coming into being of personal authority in exercising one's profession. Without the authority of experience, the professional will remain subject to the knowledge of others. In contrast to the early stages of video education, which presupposed the possibility of authority to determine useful knowledge and its optimal sequencing *a priori*, and ultimately assumed that professionals needn't even be consulted in determining the priorities for their education, what is here proposed is a set of varied approaches whose use in rotation, following tailored formulas, should enable professionals to entrench their own decision-making capabilities in confidence and freedom.

Here are the thoughts of several beginners, on completion of their video study group session:

"It provided a lot of examples. Now I have plenty of ideas for preparing activities. Organization: we learned how to get organized fast."

"It's called *participating*. We just did it. I got a lot out of working in a team, and the preparation has provided me with work techniques. I improved because it was always necessary to find new things."

"I remember that at the beginning, there was one girl on the team who had never worked, and she kept saying she had no ideas. I'm sure that today she has lots of ideas. It develops your imaginative side."

"I learned to be less shy, to represent a group, to stay ahead and be dynamic, to offer my own ideas, and to get my point across. I'd do it [this study group session] all over again, because my own main goal is my capacity to express myself. And here I'd already be ahead. I'm not shy anymore; it doesn't bother me anymore."

In Brief

I'd like to close this book with a warning about the way a video study group can get derailed. The best educational tools can be used for purposes for which they were not intended.

Initially, I hesitated about using the term "video club" because of the potential for abuse of a club for group coercion, through possible invasion of privacy. But use of the term is already entrenched.

Furthermore, video teaching actions must be subject to a code of ethics. One institutional head actually wished to make a copy of a videotape whose contents would have allowed for the dismissal of a teacher; because formal agreements had been made beforehand, the person in charge of the videotapes was able to oppose this. It's inevitable that some people will be able to divert video feedback from its educational goals. Precautions can and must be taken to prevent leadership excess and the dangers that flow from obligation or dependence. From its opening pages, this book has emphasized intrinsic motivation and cooperation.

Conclusion

You've been introduced to the educational video study group: it should serve as a locus of encounter and professionalism. Not an imposed professionalism, but an increasing appropriation of the spaces of speech in school, in the workplace, and in higher education. Shared learning of how to use this tool must serve to absorb and dispel fears, not create new ones. A video study group's goals can be jointly determined, and mentors, peer facilitators, and administrators must make a commitment to participants, who are their partners in change, not to deflect the video recording process from its pedagogical goal.

Glossary

Clinical Objectification (see also Objectification) — Semi-structured methodology using video feedback to elicit and objectively examine the empirical coming-to-awareness and mental processes that occur at the moment prior actions are presented on screen.

Interaction Profession — Any profession requiring face-to-face human interaction for its practice.

Interactor — Participant in an interaction; interlocutor of an intervenor or of another interactor.

Intervenor — Worker in a profession of social interaction and care.

Learning — The creation of new practical knowledge, not previously known, using a frame of interaction that has been set up through dialogue and that is well defined.

Microeducation — Video education centered on reduced-complexity performances conducted outside of the true occupational setting.

Objectification — Questioning and systematic internal or external information loop, aimed at making oneself aware of one's mental operations.

Other-viewing — Process of observation, evaluation, and professional development based on the screening of others' experiences recorded on video in a work setting.

Professional Change — A modification of the work methods, status, or organization of professionals, based on project development.

Professional Reflection — Progressively constructed, shared bringing-to-awareness on the personal, social, and ethical goals of professional action. A mental disposition and motivation that promote the deepening of one's identity, culture, and actions within a professional community.

Self-viewing — Process of observation, self-evaluation, and professional development based on video feedback on individual experience recorded in a work setting.

Shared Reflection — Lightly structured methodology centered on creating subjective knowledge in common. Shared reflection relies on video feedback for group stimulation of reflection concomitant to the screening of professional acts or learning acts.

Stimulated Recall — Structured methodology using video feedback to make explicit prior interactive mental processes and to classify them in an objective fashion.

Verbalization — Giving verbal form to one's thoughts — thinking aloud. Retrospective verbalization on prior interactive thoughts (stimulated recall) differs from concurrent verbalization of thoughts, concomitant to the screening of the video (for clinical objectification or shared reflection).

Video Study Group — Flexible grouping of a network of people engaged in reflective research with a view to video-assisted professionalization, development, or professional change.

Video Education — Education based on video feedback.

Video Pedagogy — The set of pedagogical approaches used in video education integrated into professional activity. Video pedagogy is a new method of professionalization, professional development, and change within business, schools, and universities.

Video Reflection — Reflection on a videotape image of one's own experience.

References

Abrami, P. C., B. Chambers, C. Poulsen, J. Howden, S. d'Apollonia, C. De Simone, K. Kastelorizios, D. Wagner, and A. Glashan. 1993. *Using cooperative learning*. Montreal, Quebec: Concordia University, The Centre for the Study of Classroom Processes.

Acheson, K. A., and M. D. Gall. 1992. *Techniques in the clinical supervision of teachers: Preservice and inservice applications*. New York and London: Longman.

Anderson, J. R., L. M. Reder, and H. A. Simon. 1996. Situated learning and education. *Educational Researcher* 25, (4): 5-11.

Apple, M. 1990. *Ideology and curriculum*. New York: Routledge.

Argyris, C. 1993. *Knowledge for action*. San Francisco: Jossey-Bass Publishers.

Barone, T. E. 1992. A narrative of enhanced professionalism: Educational researchers and popular storybooks about schoolpeople. *Educational Researcher* 21(8): 15-24.

Baxter, J. A. 1991. An evaluation of the microteaching movement in relation to cognitive approaches to the study of teaching. Paper presented at the annual meeting of the American Educational Research Association, April, Chicago.

Bellenger, L. 1981. *L'expression orale (The Oral Expression)*. Paris: ESF.

Berliner, D. 1989. The place of process-product research in developing the agenda for research on teacher thinking. In *Teacher thinking and professional action*, edited by J. Lowyck and C. M. Clark. Leuven, Belgium: Leuven University Press.

Bertrand, Y. 1995. *Contemporary theories and practice in education*. Madison, WI: Atwood Publishing.

Brophy, J., and T. Good. 1986. Teacher-effect results. In *Handbook of research on teaching*, 3rd ed., edited by M. C. Wittrock. York: MacMillan.

Carbonneau, M., and J.-C. Hétu. 1993. *La classe en direct (Classroom Live)*. Montreal, Quebec: Université de Montréal, département de psychopédagogie et andragogie.

Carroll, J. B. 1989. The Carroll Model: A 25-year retrospective and prospective view. *Educational Researcher* 18(1): 26-31.

Calgren, I., G. Handal, and S. Vaage. 1994. *Teachers' minds and actions: Research on teachers' thinking and practice*. London: Falmer Press.

Cizek, G. 1995. Crunchy granola and the hegemony of the narrative. *Educational Researcher* 24(2): 26-30.

Clandinin, J., and E. M. Connelly. 1996. Teachers' professional knowledge landscapes: Teacher stories — stories of teachers — school stories — stories of schools. *Educational Researcher* 25(3): 24-30.

Cohen, E. G. 1994a. *Designing groupwork: Strategies for the heterogeneous classroom*, 2nd ed. New York: Teachers College Press.

———. 1994b. Restructuring the classroom: Conditions for productive small groups. *Review of Educational Research* 64(1): 1-35.

Collay, M. 1991. Microteaching revisited: Through the looking glass and what Alice found there. Paper presented at the annual meeting of the American Educational Research Association, April, Chicago.

Copeland, W. D. 1993. Video cases and the thinking of preservice teachers. Paper presented at the annual meeting of the American Educational Research Association, April, Atlanta.

Darling-Hammond, L. 1996. The right to learn and the advancement of teaching: Research, policy, and practice for democratic education. *Educational Researcher* 25(6): 5-18.

Davydov, V. V. 1995. The influence of L.S. Vygotsky on education theory, research and practice. *Educational Researcher*, 24(3): 12-21.

Denzin, N. K., and Y. Lincoln. 1994. *Handbook of qualitative research.* Thousand Oaks, CA: Sage.

DeRuiter, J. A. 1991. The development of teachers' pedagogical content knowledge. Paper presented at the annual meeting of the American Educational Research Association, April, Chicago.

Devine, J. 1996. *Maximum security: The culture of violence in inner-city schools.* Chicago: University of Chicago Press.

DeVries, R. 1997. Piaget's social theory. *Educational Researcher* 26(2): 4-17.

Driver, R., H. Asoko, J. Leach, E. Mortimer, and P. Scott. 1994. Constructing scientific knowledge in the classroom. *Educational Researcher* 23(7): 5-12.

Eisner, E. W. 1988. The primacy of experience and the politics of method. *Educational Researcher* 17: 15-20.

Fenstermacher, G. D. 1990. Some moral considerations on teaching as a profession. In *The moral dimensions of teaching,* edited by J. I. Goodlad, R. Soder, and K. A. Sirotnik. San Francisco: Jossey-Bass, Publishers.

Fenstermacher, G. D., and V. Richardson. 1993. The elicitation and reconstruction of practical arguments in teaching. *Journal of Curriculum Studies* 25(2): 101-114.

Fenstermacher, G., and J. F. Soltis. 1992. *Approaches to teaching,* 2nd ed. New York: Teachers College Press.

Fetterman, D. M. 1996. Videoconferencing on-line: Enhancing communication over the Internet. *Educational Researcher* 25(4): 23-27.

Flinders, D. J. 1991. *An evaluation of the microteaching movement in relation to aesthetic, sociocultural, and feminist theories of teaching.* Paper presented at the annual meeting of the American Educational Research Association, April, Chicago.

Frederiksen, J. R., M. Sipusic, M. Gamoran, and E. Wolfe. 1992. *Video portfolio assessment: A study for the national board for professional teaching standards.* Emeryville, CA: Educational Testing Service.

Freire, P. 1997. *Mentoring the mentor: A critical dialogue with Paulo Freire.* New York: Peter Lang.

Fullan, M., and N. Watson. 1991. Beyond partnership: Supporting organizational change through school/university collaboration. Paper presented at the annual meeting of the American Educational Research Association, April, Chicago.

Gamoran Sherin, M. 1995. Teachers' content knowledge viewed across contexts. Paper presented at the annual meeting of the American Educational Research Association, April, New York.

Garrison, J. 1994. Realism, Deweyan pragmatism, and educational research. *Educational Researcher* 23(1): 5-14.

Giroux, H. 1992. *Border crossings: Cultural workers and the politics of education.* New York: Routledge.

Glaserfeld (von), E. 1995. *Radical constructivism: A way of knowing.* London: Falmer Press.

Goldman Segall, R. 1991. A multimedia research tool for ethnographic investigation. In *Constructivism* edited by I. Harel. New York: Ablex.

Gravel, S., S. Parent, and J. Tremblay. 1995. *Une nouvelle avenue vers l'optimalisation de l'enseignement et des compétences* (A new avenue toward optimal teaching and competencies). Jonquière, Quebec: CEGEP de Jonquière.

Green, M. 1994. Epistemology and educational research: The influence of recent approaches to knowledge. In *Review of research in education,* Vol. 20, edited by L. Darling-Hammond. Washington, DC: American Educational Research Association.

Hansen, E. G., and J. L. Mounty. 1995. Sign language and interactive video technology for learning, assessment, and performance support for deaf students. Paper presented at the annual meeting of the American Educational Research Association, April, New York.

Heron, J. 1996. *Co-operative inquiry: Research into the human condition.* Thousand Oaks, CA: Sage.

Holborn, P. 1992. Becoming a reflective practitioner. In *Becoming a teacher,* Vol. 2, edited by P. Holborn, M. Wideen, and I. Andrews. Montreal, Quebec: Logiques.

Hytten, K. 1997. Rethinking pragmatism: Education and the pragmatist social project. Paper presented at the annual meeting of the American Educational Research Association, March, Chicago.

Johnson, D. W., and R. T. Johnson. 1994. *Leading the cooperative school*. Edina, MN: Interaction Book.

Jones, B. F., ed. 1990. *Dimensions of thinking: A review of research*. Hillsdale, NJ: Erlbaum.

Kagan, S. 1992. *Cooperative learning*. San Juan Capistrano, CA: Resources for Teachers.

Knuth, R., and S. Baxendale. 1995. Video-based approaches for teacher development. Paper presented at the annual meeting of the American Educational Research Association, April, San Francisco.

Kulik, C. L., J. A. Kulik, and R. L. Bangert-Drowns. 1990. Effectiveness of mastery learning programs: A meta-analysis. *Review of Educational Research* 60(2): 265-307.

Latour, B. 1997. *Nous n'avons jamais été modernes: Essai d'anthropologie symétrique* (We were never modern: An essay in symmetrical anthropology). Paris: La Découverte/Sciences humaines et sociales.

Lefebvre, M.-É., and J. Poncet-Montange. 1996. La bande vidéo, outil de coconstruction d'une mémoire (Co-constructing practical memories through video). *Revue des sciences de l'éducation* 22(3): 603-622.

McLaren, P. 1991. Critical pedagogy: Constructing an arch of social dreaming and a doorway to hope. *Journal of Education* 173(1): 9-34.

Marzano, R. J., R.S. Brandt, C. S. Hugues, B. F. Jones, B. Z. Presseisen, S. C. Rankin, and C. Suhor. 1988. *Dimensions of thinking: A framework for curriculum and instruction*. Alexandria, VA: ASCD.

Munby, H., and T. Russell. 1994. The experience as authority when learning to teach: Messages from a physics class. *Journal of Teacher Education* 45(2): 86-95.

Palkiewicz, J. 1990. Développement de la pensée et de l'action responsable dans une perspective d'acquisition de compétences au collégial. Actes du 10e colloque annuel de l'Association québécoise de pédagogie collégiale, May, Québec: AQPC.

Paré, A., and M. Auclair. 1988. Vidéoscopie, visualisation et supervision pédagogique (Videoscopy, visualization and pedagogical supervision). *Recherches psychopédagogiques* 1(2): 31-37.

Penuel, W. R., and J. V. Wertsch. 1995. Vygotsky and identity formation: A sociocultural approach. *Educational Psychologist* 30(2): 83-92.

Perkins, D. 1995. *Image as insight: The role of representations in understanding.* Cambridge, MA: Harvard Graduate School of Education, Project Zero.

Phillips, D. C. 1995. The good, the bad, and the ugly: The many faces of constructivism. *Educational Researcher* 24(7): 5-12.

Pinard, W. P., W. M. Reynolds, P. Slattery, and P. M. Taubman. 1995. *Understanding curriculum.* New York: Peter Lang.

Pruyn, M. 1993. *Becoming subjects through critical practice.* Presentation, April, Los Angeles: UCLA Graduate School of Education.

Richardson, V. 1994. *Teacher change and the staff development process.* New York: Teachers College Press.

Richardson, V., and P. Heckman. 1996. Rétroaction vidéo et amitié critique: de l'explicitation des prémisses de l'expérience au changement scolaire (Video feedback and critical friendship: From the explicitation of the premises of experience to school change). *Revue des sciences de l'éducation* 22(3): 601-627.

Risko, V. J., and J. Towell. 1991. The effect of video-based case methodology on preservice teachers' problem solving and critical thinking. Paper presented at the annual meeting of the American Educational Research Association, April, Chicago.

Roche, A., A. Guiguet, and N. Voltz. 1989. *L'atelier d'écriture: éléments pour la rédaction du texte littéraire* (Writing workshop: Element for writing literary texts). Paris: Bordas.

Roschelle, J. 1995. *Video analysis tools: Keep it simple, flexible, portable.* Berkeley, CA: University of California at Berkeley, Institute for Research on Learning.

Rosenshine, B. 1997. The case for explicit, teacher-led, cognitive strategy instruction. Paper presented at the annual meeting of the American Educational Research Association, March, Chicago.

Rosenshine, B., and C. Meister. 1994. Reciprocal teaching: A review of the research. *Review of Educational Research* 64(4): 479-530.

Saunders, C., and O. Hargie. 1989. The effects of video feedback on students' evaluation of self. *Journal of Educational Television* 15(3): 143-153.

Saunders, S. 1992. The nature of preservice teachers' comments in discussing a videotaped teaching case. Paper presented at the annual meeting of the American Educational Research Association, April, San Francisco.

Schoenfeld, A. H. 1985. *Mathematical problem solving.* New York: Academic Press.

Schoenfeld, A. H., M. Gamoran, M. Leonard, C. Kessel, R. Orbach, and A. Arcavi. 1993. Toward a comprehensive model of human tutoring in complex subject matter domains. *Journal of Mathematical Behavior* 11(4): 1-22.

Schön, D. A. 1991. *The reflective turn: Case studies in and on educational practice.* New York: Teachers College Press.

Solomon, G., D. N. Perkins, and T. Globerson. 1991. Partners in cognition: Extending human intelligence with intelligent technologies. *Educational Researcher* 20(3): 2-9.

Sternberg, R. J., and J. A. Horvath. 1995. A prototype view of expert teaching. *Educational Researcher* 24(6): 9-18.

Tochon, F. V. 1994. Presence beyond the narrative: Semiotic tools for deconstructing the personal story. *Curriculum Studies* 2(2): 221-247.

Tochon, F. V., and J.-P. Dionne. 1994. Discourse analysis and Instructional flexibility: A pragmatic grammar. *Pragmatics and Language Learning, Monograph Series* 5: 64-87.

Tochon, F. V., and P. Trudel, eds. 1996. La rétroaction vidéo en recherche et en formation (Video feedback in research and education). *Revue des sciences de l'éducation,* numéro thématique, 22(3).

Tomlinson, P. 1995. *Understanding mentoring: Reflective strategies for school-based teacher preparation.* Philadelphia: Open University Press.

Trudel, P. 1995. Regards sur la pratique pédagogique (A glance at pedagogical practice). *Vie pédagogique* 93: 5-6.

Trudel, P., J. Côté, and D. Bernard. 1996. Systematic observation of youth ice hockey coaches during games. *Journal of Sport Behaviors* 19: 50-66.

Trudel, P., L. Haughian, and W. Gilbert. (1996). L'utilisation de la technique du rappel stimulé pour mieux comprendre le processus d'intervention de l'entraîneur en sport (Using stimulated recall to better understand the educational process of sport coaching). *Revue des sciences de l'éducation (Review of Educational Sciences)* 22(3): 505-524.

Vare, J. W. 1993. Co-constructing the zone: A neo-Vygotskian view of micro-teaching. Paper presented at the annual meeting of the American Educational Research Association, April, Atlanta.

Villeneuve, L. 1994. *L'encadrement du stage supervisé* (Supervision of the supervised practicum). Montreal, Quebec: Éditions Saint-Martin.

Woods, B. S., and P. K. Murphy. 1997. Thickening the discussion: Inspecting constructivist theories of knowledge through a Jamesian lens. Paper presented at the annual meeting of the American Educational Research Association, March, Chicago.

Zeichner, K. M. 1994. Research on teacher thinking and different views of reflective practice in teaching and teacher education. In *Teachers' minds and actions: Research on teachers' thinking and practice*, edited by I. Carlgren, G. Handal, and S. Vaage, S. London: Falmer Press.

About the Author

Born in 1954, François Victor Tochon holds a doctorate in didactics (Laval University) and a doctorate in educational psychology (University of Ottawa). For twenty years, he has been active as a facilitator and teacher educator. He taught at the University of Geneva and the University of Manitoba before coming to the University of Sherbrooke (Quebec), where he is a full professor. François Victor Tochon has been a visiting professor at Brussels University, the University of Toronto, Paris 5, Nanterre, the University of Hanoi, and Princeton University. He has published a dozen books and over a hundred scholarly articles and book chapters which have won him international recognition.